The Enlightenment Abolished

Citizens of Britishness

1562 - 1807 - 1834 - 1838

People are not just 'races'
named and ranked by man:
People are people...

GEOFF PALMER

Published in association with

Henry Publishing

ISBN No. 0-9549519-0-5

1st print re-issue

Copies can be ordered from
www.henrypublishing.co.uk

or:

Henry Publishing,
23 Waulkmill Drive, Penicuik EH26 8LA
Midlothian, Scotland, UK.

Printed by Tempus IME Ltd, Tel: 0131 516 5678, Web: www.tempusime.com

Contents

Dedication

And the old man said:
"Our slavery was not life -
It was an unjust stain
that only equality will remove"

DEDICATION

The Enlightenment Abolished is dedicated to Reverend Robert Wedderburn. He was born into slavery in 1762 in Jamaica and died in England in 1835. He was the son of James Wedderburn of Inveresk, Scotland and Wedderburn's black slave, Rosanna. Robert Wedderburn was rejected by his father who turned him away from his house, Inveresk Lodge, which was bought with 27 years of slave-money acquired in Jamaica. Robert Wedderburn raged against the injustice and degradation of slavery. He was jailed in London for his anti-slavery protests. However, his father James Wedderburn lived out his post-slavery life, in great luxury in Inveresk.

James Wedderburn's house, Inveresk Lodge, now stands in Trust, in its whitewash splendour at the high end of a large tranquil garden, now open to all. Local historians speak graciously about James Wedderburn and his well-placed white descendants but, through either ignorance or omission, no mention is made of his 27 years as a rapacious slave-owner in Jamaica. James Wedderburn did not invite his son Robert Wedderburn into his house at Inveresk Lodge in 1795. However, in 2003 Lord Bill Wedderburn, the distinguished scholar, and his wife Lady Frances Wedderburn and I were allowed inside the Lodge. Time and endeavour enabled us to complete what Robert Wedderburn had intended to do in 1795. Lord (Professor) Wedderburn is a proud descendant of the slave Robert Wedderburn. Both he and Frances came back to Inveresk Lodge in 2007, to participate in the commemoration of the 200th anniversary of the Abolition of the British Slave Trade. *The Robert Wedderburn Walk* was staged by a large diverse group of people to honour and remember the pilgrimage made by Robert Wedderburn in 1795 (article 17). Sadly, Lord Bill Wedderburn passed away in 2012.

Biography

THE AUTHOR

Geoff Henry Palmer is Professor Emeritus of Grain Science at the Heriot Watt University, Edinburgh and has received various awards for his research and community work (Articles 49, 54, 55). Recently he not only received a distinguished research award as a grain scientist from the American Society of Brewing Chemists, he was also awarded the Sir William Y. Darling bequest from The Edinburgh City Council for his work in "race relations", the OBE (Order of the British Empire) for his research contribution to grain science and the "Black Champion" award for notable contribution to the community in 2002, 2003 and 2004 respectively. In 2005 Professor Palmer was elected Professor Emeritus of the Heriot Watt University, Edinburgh in Scottish-Diaspora Home Coming year (2009) he was awarded a Honorary Degree of Doctor of Science by the University of Abertay, Dundee in the presence of The High Commissioner of Jamaica, His Excellency The Honourable Burchell Whiteman. Also in 2009, he was awarded an additional Honorary Doctorate in Arts and Science by the Open University (55). These degrees complement his Research Degree of Doctor of Science which was achieved in 1983. He regards this narrative as an attempt to show the terrible consequences of slavery, ignorance and prejudice. Examples of his work on these topics are presented in newspaper articles referenced and reproduced below.

These were written to inform our education and justice systems of some of the difficulties Black-British children face in this society. Despite a large 'race relations industry' many of these problems remain…maybe new approaches are required to remove the erroneous perception that black people have not and do not contribute to the good image and wealth of the country. His recently published short story, 'Mr White and the Ravens' (ISBN: 0-9549519-1-3). Henry Publishing, Scotland, is a new or alternative approach at showing the social damage that can be caused by imperialistic ideology based on ignorance and prejudice (articles 13, 14, 19).

Professor Palmer maintains that the anomalous word 'race' is judgemental, divisive, scientifically meaningless and reinforces prejudice. Its origins and meaning are uncertain. It is divisive and should, in future, be abolished and never be applied to human beings. Surely, identical hearts are more important than differences in skin colour. However, in this narrative, it is used as expected. In terms of logic, it is nonsense to refer to 'races of people' and retain the concept of Human race. Instead of using the phrase 'race relations', we should concentrate our efforts on improving Human relations. In contrast to the word race, the word Human provides a more accurate description of our equality as people. That a large group of white teachers, to whom Professor Palmer was lecturing, declined to define the word race suggests that they were either ignorant of the word or afraid of its politics…no one should be put in such a position in any society.

Professor Palmer believes that 'equal opportunity' is a pointless concept if people do not have the means to realise opportunities. Education should be used to ensure and secure rights. However, if education fails the law cannot afford to fail (50). He hopes that others, who work in this area, will do all they can to educate those who would deny the rights of other human beings. Finally the author thanks many people for support: Family, friends, Craig Nicol for design and print input, the Jamaican Archive and those who sent the surprising but encouraging responses to the publication, 'Mr White and the Ravens'. Professor Palmer's optimism regarding human affinity is derived from the view that politically, it has always been very destructive to keep people apart anywhere in the world.

ARTICLES:

1. 'Where Children are Still Seen and Not Heard' (page 128) ,
The Times Educational Supplement, 20.3.1970

2. 'No Kill Nobody but a Policeman',
The Times Educational Supplement, 16.10.1970

3. 'Handsworth: Caribbean Black Country' (page 133),
The Times Educational Supplement, 16.6.1972 **(*Postscript* 2004)**

4. 'Breaking Away for the Black Stereotype',
Geoff Palmer speaking to Colleen Williams
The Weekly Gleaner, 15.8.1986

5. 'Multicultural Education',
Church of Scotland report to the General Assembly:
*Committee on Education Report to Board of Education
(response to Swann's "Education for All") Chaired by G.H.Palmer,
Edinburgh, 1990*

6. 'Food for Thought in a Multicultural Britain' (page 144),
Sunday Express, 25.6.2000

7. 'Brewing up a Storm',
Geoff Palmer speaking to Kenneth Taylor
The Voice, 17 and 24.12.2001

8. 'Punished for being Jamaican'...new Visa Regime (page 148),
The Edinburgh Evening News, 25.1.2003

9. 'Education Race and Citizenship' (page 153)
School of the Divinity, Centre for Theology and Public Issues
Edinburgh University, 2004

10. Robert Wedderburn:
'Disowned by his Father...for the Colour of His Skin',
Geoff Palmer speaking to Sandra Dick
Edinburgh Evening News, 9.6.2003

11. 'Go Back and Grow Bananas',
Geoff Palmer speaking to Olga Wojtas
Times Higher Educational Supplement, 15.8.2003

12. 'The Race to Open Our Borders and Our Minds'
Geoff Palmer speaking to Tom Lynch,
The Sunday Times, 29.4.2004

13. 'My Colour Is Me'
(Based on article, Freedom Colour Prejudice (page 158)
Geoff Palmer
Black Information Link, website, 26.2.2007

14. 'The Registrar-General and the Black and White Question
in Scotland', Geoff Palmer
The Herald, 20.3.2007

15. 'Still Fighting for Freedom'
Geoff Palmer speaking to Cassandra Jardine,
The Daily Telegraph, 22.3.2007

16. 'Walkers to Remember Strides Taken by Anti-slavery Activist'
(page 161) Geoff Palmer speaking to Adrian Mather,
Edinburgh Evening News, 23.4.2007

17. 'The 200th year Commemoration of the Abolition of the
British Slave Trade in the West Indies: 1807-2007' (page 6) Robert
Wedderburn Freedom Walk: From Musselburgh High Street to
Inveresk Lodge. Geoff Palmer:
Written for the National Trust for Scotland, 2007

18. 'Geoff Palmer' Interviewed by Gavin D Smith
Scotch Whisky Review, Spring, 2007

19. 'Wicked Commerce', Geoff Palmer
Black London Magazine, Bicentennial Edition, April, 2007.

20. 'House sale is linked to dark era in Scottish history' (letter
regarding multi-milion pound sale in 2008 of Fasque House,
Scotland...the (1829 purchased) house of the notorious slave owner,
Sir John Gladstone, father of prime minister, William Gladstone)
Geoff Palmer
The Scotsman, 04.03.2008

21. 'Scotland's role in 300 years of slavery', interviewed by Leroy Carter. *West Lothian Times*, 8.1.2008

22. 'Scottish Caribbeans are an important part of the country's complex history', Geoff Palmer
The Herald, 10.11.2008

23. 'Tartan and home truths, A new centre for the study of the Scottish diaspora is already caught up in controversy', Interviewed by Jackie Kemp.
The Guardian, 25.11.2008

24. 'Do not forget role of Scots in slave trade', interviewed by Mike Wade. *The Times*, 8.12.2008

25. 'How Capital life helped Darwin's theory to evolve', interviewed by Laura Cummings with regard to ex-slave John Edmonstone teaching Darwin Taxidermy at Edinburgh University.
Evening News, 3.2.2009

26. 'Why a discrepancy in alcohol-related illness?' *The Herald*, 27.05.2010

27. 'Alcohol problem has a strong localised base that defies one-sided evidence!'
The Herald, 10.06.2010

28. 'Time for a sober look at alcohol', *Evening News*, Edinburgh, 23.8.2010

29. 'Poor evidence' (on alcohol management), The Scotsman, Letter to the Editor, Professor Emeritus Geoff Palmer, 6.9.2010

30. 'Holistic approach' (on alcohol management), The Scotsman, Letter to the Editor, Professor Emeritus Geoff Palmer, 20.9.2010

31. The Z Files, Youtube, Professor Geoff Palmer. Benjamin Zephaniah interviews Professor Geoff Palmer (in support of The Open University's aim to encourage black children to pursue careers in science), 24. 9.2010

32. 'Jamaican scientist opens door for African-Caribbean children', The Guardian, Jackie Kemp interviews Professor Geoff Palmer, 30.9.2010

33. 'Stephen Lawrence Analysis: Society is more mixed but racism has not gone away – we still have a long way to go', *The Scotsman*, 5.1.2012.

34. 'Black and Minority Ethnic (BME), STEM (Science, Technology, Engineering and Maths) and University Education, *Newsletter, Edinburgh and Lothian's Regional Equality Council,* Edinburgh, April. 2012.

35. 'Ode to Glasgow. Glasgow:

The city where seagulls stand on great men's heads
And sparrows fight bigger birds for bread...and win.

The Herald, 7.5.2012.

36. 'Drink policy ought to apply to affluent as well as poor', *The Herald,* 17.5. 2012.

37. 'Other solutions to drink abuse needed', *The Scotsman,* 17.5.2012.

38. 'Vodka impact', *The Scotsman,* 24.7.2012.

39. 'Prof. Palmer requests' (grains for his new pre-germination test), *Brewer & Distiller International,* volume 8, issue 8, August 2012.

40. 'Report on the Educational Progression of Children from Black Minority Ethnic (BME) and Deprived Communities', Professor Geoff Palmer, *Issue 33 – Edinburgh and Lothian Regional Equality Council Newsletter*, October 2012. Pages 2 and 10

41. 'Politicians using slavery to make a point is offensive', Letter to Edinburgh Evening News (also, see news.scotsman.com), Friday 8th March, 2013.

42. BBC, Radio 4. The Listening Project.
You changed my life: Reginald to Geoff. 3rd June 2013.

43. BBC, Radio Scotland, Sunday Morning with Ricky Ross,
*Discussion about Martin Luther King's, "I have a dream" speech. 25th
August 2013.*

44. St Andrew's Day Lecture: "It wisnae us", Lecture on Scottish
involvement in British chattel slavery in the New World, by Rev
Richard Holloway (Chair), Professor Geoff Palmer and Professor
Tom Devine, Edinburgh University, 30.11.2013.

45. 'Other factors in liver disease', Letter to The Herald, 23.12.
2013.

46. BBC Radio, "Life Story" Sunday Morning with Cathy
Macdonald (Part 1), 12.1.2014.

47. Sir Keith's insult, The Spectator letters, 26th September
2015.

48. Palmer vs Moore, Agriculture and Sir Keith, The Spectator
letters, 10th October 2015.

49. 'Migrants ought to be given a chance to shine', Mike Wade,
The Times, 5th September 2015: See Article 11.

50. Race Relations in the next fifty years must be fairer that it is
today, Edinburgh and Lothian Regional Equality Council, Issue
45, November 2015, page 4.

51. Row over Heriot – Watt University academic Sir Geoff
Palmer 'bananas' claim against Tory on BBC Radio 4, The
Herald, David Leask, 14th September, 2015: See Article 11.

52. 'Mrs Thatcher's intellectual guru faces extraordinary claims
he told Jamaican – born man to 'go back and grow bananas',
Eleanor Harding, Daily Mail, 10th September, 2015.

53. 'Go home and study bananas', Anne Widdecombe, Daily
Express, 16th September 2015

54. 'University drinks a toast to first black professor', The Scotsman, Brian Pendreigh, 28th November, 1992.

55. Notices: Honorary Doctorate Degrees (2015): Heriot Watt University, Edinburgh: University of the West Indies and University of Technology, Jamaica: Leicester University, 2016.

56. Palmer G H (2016) Beverages: Distilled. Wrigley, C., Corke, H., Seetharaman, K. and Faubion, J. (eds), *Encyclopedia of Food Grains*, 2nd Edition, pp 193-205, Oxford, Academic Press.

57. Palmer G H (2017) Jamaica, Modification, Justice, Industry – (Requested) Autobiography of my scientific life and work, Journal of the American Society of Brewing Chemist, In the press.

58. See comments in: This is truth about tyrant's slave trade past. To deny it is height of nonsense, Mark Aitkin, Sunday Mail, August, 27, 2017. Scotland's Dirty Money, Murray Scougall, Sunday Post, October 1, 2017.

TELEVISION AND FILM CONTRIBUTIONS:

BBC 2: Andrew Watson, the 19th Century black football captain of Scotland, 2003.

BBC 2: 'The Scottish Empire', Programme 2 (West Indian Slavery), Wark Clements Production, 2004.

Jamaica television interview (JIS) by Ian Boyne, Jamaican achievers, 2005.

BBC: www.bbc.co.uk/scotland/education/hist/abolition, September, 2007.

Media Trust, 2012: On the internet: Video and DVD, The age old excuse', to support Macmillan cancer charity.

CVM Television - Under 21 Netball Team donates 18th Century map to National Library 2013 (Google), see page 128.

Scotland Tonight: should our slave past be taught in Schools?
STV (9.1.2014), BBC1 – The One Show. Scotland's Slavery
(16.01.2014).

BBC, Radio 4, Life Scientific, 4th August 2015.

STV History programme, Scotland and Slavery, June 26, 2017

Videos, Twitter and You Tube, Scotland and the Slave Trade:
Henry Dundas. Urquhart media, October 2017.

In the New Year's Honours List of 2014 Professor Geoff Palmer
received the Higher Award of Knight Bachelor. Professor Sir Godfrey
(Geoff) Palmer was given the award for work done in the areas of
Science, Human Rights and Charity.

Without *system consciousness,* failure in society is certain...

Knowing should lead to understanding.

For who would bear the whips and scorns of time,

The oppressor's wrong, the proud man's contumely,

The pangs of dispriz'd love, the law's delay,

The insolence of office...

Shakespeare

Whatever mitigates the woes or increases the happiness of others,

this is my criterion of goodness; and whatever injures society at

large or any individual in it, this is my measure of iniquity...

Burns

But someday, somebody'll

stand up and talk about me

and write about me

black and beautiful

and sing about me

and put on plays about me!

I reckon it'll be

me myself!

Yes, it'll be me.

Hughes

† †
834   Montego-Bay, Dec 14, 1790.
FOR SALE,
On Thurſday the 23d inſtant,
439 Prime, Healthy, Young, Eboe
NEGROES,
Imported in the Ship
BROTHERS,
Captain JOSEPH WITHERS,
From BONNY.
James Wedderburn & Co.
† †

The Present and the Future go together...

Preface To Slavery

BRITISH CHATTEL SLAVERY: THE ABOLITION OF THE BRITISH SLAVE TRADE (1807)

We are the descendants of black Chattel slaves that were giants. They gave us their lives to live with honour.

In 1807, when the British Slave Trade was abolished, Lord Granville, the Prime Minister, remarked that in years to come Britain may be 'reproached' for a slavery which was a 'mischief'. According to an earlier Prime Minister (1783), Lord North, British slavery was economically 'necessary'. Henry Dundas (Lord Melville), the powerful politician that controlled British slavery (1790-1806) when Pitt was Prime Minister, stated that British slavery, because of its economic importance to Britain, will be 'gradually' abolished. Dundas frustrated Wilberforce's efforts to abolish the Slave Trade for nearly fifteen years. If we put these views together we have a sad explanation of how some people, during *The Enlightenment*, reasoned that slavery should not be abolished and that there ought to be no guilt regarding British slavery. The basis of this reasoning was that, this slavery was a mischief and, by definition, a mischief has no malice. Therefore, the cynical excuse for a terrible slavery, sanctioned by British law, was: no malice…no guilt. In this context, the Church accepted this political excuse and consolidated it by stating that slavery and abolition were in the hands of God while profiting from this slavery. Politically, slavery was abolished, not because of guilt but because industrial development, in Britain, after 1832, was becoming more profitable than an increasingly rebellious and troublesome slavery, thousands of miles away, in the Caribbean. It is therefore not surprising that Buxton, a Member of Parliament and a rich industrial brewer of moral conscience, was selected by

Wilberforce in 1823 to bring about the Emancipation of British slaves which occurred in 1833-1834. 'Slave laws' and language such as 'necessary', 'gradually' and 'mischief' were used to absolve and exonerate those who carried out the most profitable evil the world has known. It is therefore not surprising that many slavers saw themselves as worthy citizens and men of God. Indeed, James Baillie, a notorious Scottish slaver (1793), referred to abolitionists as 'ignorant and low men'…such is the complexity of a brutal slavery that took hundreds of years to abolish. Indeed, this slavery was Chattel slavery and it produced a prejudice that has been used to denigrate Black people for centuries. However, ironically, it will be shown that although this slavery, in terms of the words Chattel slavery, was not usually mentioned in British tourist brochures and even books, it is the slavery to which social problems in the world are compared frequently to gain attention, without clarification or respect. Thankfully, the historical amnesia that suppressed the history of British chattel slavery has given way to an enlightened history that is welcomed by the people because it deals with the causes and effects of an important period of the history of the world.

During the commemoration of the 200th anniversary of the abolition of the British slave trade it has been stated, in various quarters, that Chattel slavery, to which the slaves of the West Indies were subjected, is similar to human trafficking, indentured labour or even Clearance of the Scottish Highlands (1746). This argument of denial has been used to dilute the brutal slavery to which our ancestors were subjected for over three hundred years. Some people have refused to take part in the commemoration because, although they readily glorify the good deeds of their ancestors, they are slow to acknowledge the crimes they committed. Curiously, these are the people who want us to "learn" British history. Is Chattel slavery not British history?

The British (Barbados) Chattel Slave Code (1661), adopted as the Slave Code in America, was used to great effect by British slave masters: It required by law that, all slaves should be clothed. However, it also denied slaves basic human rights guaranteed under British law such as the right to life. It allowed slave owners to do entirely as they wished to their slaves, including mutilating them and burning them alive, without fear of reprisal. This also meant that the children of slaves belonged to slave masters and they were sold by them. White slave masters often freed their mixed race children but also had the right to sell them. The British Slave Code meant that *a slave master could legally kill his slave*. If you have no human rights, only then can you be called a Chattel slave. Therefore, when Luke Collingwood, Captain of the British slave ship the Zong, threw his slaves overboard and drowned them in 1781, to gain the insurance, he was tried but found not guilty of murder. He had not broken British 'slave laws'; the judge ruled that the slaves Collingwood had killed were Chattel, not human beings. Collingwood was therefore found not guilty of murder. Is this equivalent to the injustices of trafficking ("modern slavery"), which is not legal? To compare trafficking to Chattel slavery is an insult to the millions of black people that died as British slaves. There can be no religious, biological, philosophical or moral excuse for the unacceptable legal contrivance at Collingwood's trial. Human beings are human beings not animals: no-one could have failed to recognise this.

It is worrying that the commemorations will pass and the horror of Chattel slavery will not be understood because many of the books, articles and official documents do not mention the word Chattel thereby understating the brutality of New World slavery. After giving a lecture to children on Chattel slavery and illustrating it with the case of the *Zong* a teenager in the audience said, "I can understand why the captain threw the sick slaves overboard, but it was a waste that he drowned the healthy slaves too." If this is the nature of our moral education in schools, the unthinking response of those who would deny British slavery is understandable. At the end of another lecture, a Minister of the Church said that although he was familiar with African history he was unaware of Scotland's involvement in British slavery. In a letter, another Minister regarded the documented life of Robert Wedderburn as a "tale" and objected to people knowing that his town had an association with slavery. He also remarked that the images of slavery were too upsetting for the town's children to see...but in an unprincipled way failed to consider the children of slaves who had to watch the brutality. Nevertheless, to show he was a man of God and mercy he added in his letter that he would give some pulpit time to human trafficking ("modern slavery"). Why? Is it because "modern slavery" carries no 'sins' to which he can be connected? Such is the poor regard for our section of British history that the truth about its slavery can be dismissed cynically as a...bad historical tale. Indeed, when I stated to a Professor from Hull University that he should have used his Rowntree grant money to compare British Chattel Slavery with "modern slavery" rather than compare "British Slavery with "modern slavery", he promised clarification but failed to respond. He was fully aware that his proposal, that "British Slavery" was the same as "modern slavery", was a lie to promote the trafficking campaign. Trafficking is wrong but for an academic to misrepresent the meaning of Chattel slavery is disgraceful.

Sadly, this lack of respect is indeed the subject of a recent letter cited in Article 41 at the beginning of this book. The letter refers to a Scottish politician who, in 2013, distastefully used the words 'slavery' and 'massah' to attract attention to his party and himself without realising that the slavery to which he referred was, in part, owned and managed by his ancestors for his benefit. There is no mistake regarding the slavery to which he alluded. However, in general, I was more concerned with his ignorance of his own history than with the 'racial' denigration expressed. Sadly, the politician, who has resigned form his party, is not alone in his indifference to the feelings of others. In different quarters the word 'slavery' is still being used to promote indentured 'white slavery' in the context of 'Chattel slavery', to gain support for political causes. This dishonest disregard for historical truth is an insult to those who died horrific legal deaths in 'British chattel slavery'.

A reprehensible tactic of racists is to frustrate justice for others by saying, "Others suffered too..." It is wrong to link one evil with another because doing so diminishes both evils. Each evil requires separate attention. Deception and ignorance that masquerade as balance or compassion is malicious and destructive. I have the conscience to respect the history of others...what kind of conscience must racists have to deny the history and identity of other people?

Before progressing with this narrative on British slavery, it is regrettable that in the year of remembering the holocaust of British Chattel slavery in the West Indies, civil servants in Scotland, England and Wales have initiated a process to abolish the categories, black and white from census forms. The final objective is to remove black and white from all official documents. The removal of white is a deceptive palliative because white people are not abused because of their colour and their needs are the best met in our diverse society. In contrast, the removal of black will increase racial abuse of black people and eliminate the means by which colour prejudice is monitored. The excuses given for this untimely attempt to remove the identity of black people are that a small group of Africans, not "Africans in Scotland" as reported, find the category black insulting and, to white people, black means "power". Both reasons are presented without valid scientific evidence. However, I would have thought that "white" portrays more power than "black" in our society.

In many ways the actions of these civil servants are prejudicial and are likely to damage race relations. I stated these views in an article to the Black Information Link and in a letter to The (Glasgow) Herald newspaper (see articles 13 and 14). I regarded it as astonishing that, in the year of the commemoration of the abolition of the slave trade the black identity of the descendants of British slavery is being questioned without their consent. This unequal action of our civil servants merges into institutional racism. It is also being proposed that black people should be called "Africans" and white people should be called "Europeans". That such dangerous nonsense could be distributed by civil servants without government approval is frightening. Somehow, black West Indian identity will be abolished, so will white African identity...

The vast majority of Africans, West Indians whom I know are not ashamed of their black colour and were not, like myself, consulted regarding the concept of abolishing black and white. The tampering with colour identities of black and white people is intended to please a small group of Africans...this excuse defies understanding and a more serious explanation must be given for the cost incurred and the damage done, especially to the dignity of black people. The indecent haste with which this was done should be questioned because such haste has never been applied to addressing the social, educational or medical needs of black people.

A long time ago in the 16th Century, the identity of the Moors of Africa was interchangeable, linguistically, with the identity of Black. The intention of a host of 'racists and one-directional people' to belittle Black identity, over many centuries, has failed because identity is based on life experiences not skin colour. Life-history is about identity, land is about nationality. In this context, Black is my identity and this will not change.

The negative image created about black people caused them to be enslaved. It took many great black people such as Garvey, Sengor, Hughes, Malcolm X, King, Rosa Parks, Baldwin, Kenyatta, Nkrumah, Biko and Mandela to make black dignified and beautiful again. Human beings have the right to define their own identities. My identity is black Jamaican and I have the genetic and legal right to live in Scotland and in any other part of Britain. Many West Indians can claim Scottish heritage...they already have the family names. My black lineage stems from the New World (Jamaican) slavery of my ancestors. I have no legal right to live in Africa but I am proud of my historical links with Africa. All human beings should be proud of their association with Africa...

because we all came from Africa. Notwithstanding, it still remains beyond all forms of reason to understand why a band of white civil servants would want black people of independent West Indian nations to call themselves Africans. I cannot see why anyone should ask a Kenyan or Nigerian to become a Jamaican or a Guyanese. No black person will sign or barter away the lineage and freedom of his or her black identity (Interestingly, The British Council of Muslims which is an organisation of diverse people has stated that the census categories, black and white, should be retained). Now, it is evident that the murderous journey, from the 15th century introduction of black Chattel slavery, to its legal abolition in the 19th century, is a historical journey we should all know because the consequences of this brutal slavery are still with us today.

When did black slavery begin? In 1444 the Portuguese took black people from Africa and forced them to work in Portugal. In 1455, the Pope ruled that "infidel people" should be "reduced to servitude". In 1456 the Portuguese took the Cape Verde islands and introduced slaves to plant sugar cane and make sugar. Columbus's discovery of the New World in 1492 gave Spain a very large colonial Empire to grow cane and other valuable crops. Sugar, rum, coffee, spices and cotton soon became part of the rich life-style of Europe...and for hundreds of years were the objects of bitter wars. The British, French, Spanish, Dutch, Danish and Portuguese fought each other at sea for pieces of the New World on which they could force black slaves to produce their goods. In 1553, Sir William Cecil, the English politician, stated that effective occupation was the determinant of sovereignty. Therefore the British, like other European nations, started to acquire, by conquest or discovery, colonies in the New World.

By 1553, the European Chattel slave industry was in place. In 1562 John Hawkins started the British slave trade business with the blessings of his Queen, Elizabeth I. The ingredients of this slave industry were land, black slaves, unpaid labour and merciless slave masters, in a hurry to be rich. The profit was money, as much as possible, in the shortest possible time. Nothing can stop greed with a gun. The most powerful nations in the world, Britain, France, Spain, Portugal, and the Dutch controlled half a world of slaves that was 5,000 miles away in the West Indies. Never in the history of the world were so many naval wars fought for one area of the world. The British Navy was at its most powerful and Naval Captains such as Benbow, Rodney, Nelson, Howe, Hood, Bligh, Duckworth, Wallis, Vincent and others are now part of the elite history of the British Navy because they protected the British Slave Empire in the New World. At the end of the seven years war in 1763, Britain took the slave colonies it wanted...it kept and took those best suited to grow sugar and coffee. As part of the tradition of defending British interests in the West Indies, Horatio Nelson honed his fighting skills in the West Indies. His many duties in the West Indies resulted in his marriage being held in Barbados where he was stationed. During slavery Britain lost more men fighting in the West Indies than it lost fighting in Europe over the same period. Chattel slavery was important to the British economy and no attempt to abolish it before it had run its course would have been tolerated by the British Parliament. That is why British slavery in the New World lasted nearly 300 years...the abolition movements came at the end of this very long silence of injustice.

The economic importance of British slavery was so well established that even a radical poet such as Robert Burns thanked Admiral

Rodney for defending Jamaica from the French and the Spanish at the Battle of the Saints (also called, The Battle of the Glorious 12th of April) in 1782. This was the beating in the West Indies that "softened up" the French, for Lord Nelson to defeat at Trafalgar in 1805. Jamaica had to be defended. At that period Jamaica was the most important sugar producing country in the British Empire. It was also the main destination of British (mainly English and Scottish) fortune hunters. Although poorly educated, part of my training in Britishness in secondary school in Jamaica, was to repeat Admiral Benbow's gallantry and Rodney's victory. I have met only one white British person who knew of Rodney's victory or its importance in British history. For winning this pivotal battle against France and Spain, Rodney was elevated to the Peerage and given a pension of about £2,000,000, at today's money value. Therefore, when we commemorate the abolition of the slave trade, it should not be forgotten that it took nearly three hundred years for the British Parliament to be told, collectively, that its slavery of black people was inhuman and wrong. Before 1782, The Church and the Nation benefited in silence as many millions of slaves suffered and died. The Church of England owned slaves and branded SOCIETY on their chests, the Church of Scotland did not petition for abolition and excluded slaves from its church services in Jamaica during slavery. The other churches spoke to slaves such as Sam Sharpe (1831) whose Christianity assisted his determination to fight for freedom. Sharpe was a Baptist, so were Bogle and Gordon. The Baptist Church came to Jamaica in 1814. In the face of injustice, silence is the great evil.

The New World slave plantation system was based on the economic premise that large quantities of cultivatable land that produced desirable products, with free labour, would be extremely profitable. First it was thought that the native Indians or white indentured labourers would provide free or cheap labour respectively. This was not successful. The slaving practice of the Portuguese was adopted. Based on prejudice alone, it was decided that black slaves from Africa would produce more work in the inhospitable conditions of New World Plantations. Indentured labourers had agreements which limited their working hours and time. They were also paid. Killing them or their children was a crime. The "bonus" of using black slaves was that they would not be paid and they could be worked to death.

There have been numerous academic arguments that paid work is more profitable than "slave" labour. Even if working practice is inefficient, a large free source of forced labour is infinitely more profitable than any other kind of labour. Even Adam Smith (1723 – 1790), the father of capitalism, admitted that this concept was correct. He stated that: *The profits of a sugar plantation in any of our West Indian colonies are generally much greater than those from any other civilisation known either in Europe or America.* The "free" slave labour to which Smith also refers in some of his writings pertains to white "slave by name" labour ...not Chattel slavery. Chattel slavery embodied forced wage-free labour. This practice made British slavery in the West Indies, the most profitable evil the world has known. Charles Davenant (1656 – 1714) the English economist said that, every white person from the British Islands in the West Indies brought in £10 (£1,000 at today's value) clear annual profit to England; twenty times as much as a similar person in the Home Counties of England. William Pitt (1759 – 1806), the British Prime Minister, asserted in 1798 that, the annual income from the West Indian plantations was £4 million (about £400,000,000 at today's value) compared with £1 million (about £100,000,000) from the rest of the world. Nearly two-thirds of this (£400,000,000) came from Jamaica alone (pages 120,122).

To secure an efficient supply of slaves for the production of sugar, cotton, coffee, spices and rum an efficient supply of slaves was required. John Hawkins, a merchant/adventurer, with the encouragement of Elizabeth 1, started the British slave trade by capturing black slaves in Africa and selling them in the New World, in 1562. Many more merchants/adventurers joined the trade. To make the trade more profitable, The Royal African Company was set up in 1660 by the Royal Stuart family and reformed in 1672. It was headed by the brother of Charles II...James II. Its business purpose was to purchase or capture "Negro" slaves to supply the plantations of the New World. A slave bought from an African trader for £2 could be sold for £60 into slavery. The efficiency in securing and transporting slaves was increased after the dissolution of the Royal African Company in 1698. This new free trade transported over 2 million slaves between 1680 and 1786.

Between 1700 and 1800, there were about 11,000 slave-ship sailings from London, Bristol and Liverpool. Sailings from Scotland increased many fold over this period. Article 4 of the Act of the Union of the Scottish and English Parliaments gave the Scots permission to enter the profitable English slave market which took Scotland out of poverty. After the signing of the Political Acts of the Union, Scots not only entered West Indian slavery, they also established business interest in Chesapeake in Virginia, America. By 1740 the tobacco trade in Chesapeake was dominated by Glasgow tobacco merchants. They became very rich trading tobacco grown by slaves. Many were millionaires and invested money in the development of Glasgow. Some of Glasgow's streets still bear their surnames: Buchanan, Ingram and Glasford. Grand institutes such as the Free Church of Scotland and constructions such as Virginia Buildings and William Cunninghame's house, which is the exquisite part of the Gallery of Modern Art, were both built with money gained from slavery. As Tobacco lords, Buchanan, Ingram, Spiers, Glasford and Cunninghame, like other Tobacco lords, exuded great power in Glasgow. In contrast to the Tobacco lords, James Ewing (1775-1853) was a Sugar baron (in his time, the best known public figure in Glasgow). He inherited large sugar plantations in Jamaica and initiated the building of the Glasgow Necropolis (1828) and is buried there, next to the giant statue of John Knox.

The fortunes of the Tobacco lords declined rapidly at the beginning of the American Revolution in 1775. The Americans started to manage their own tobacco trade. Tobacco lords such as Cunninghame shifted from tobacco to sugar. He had a large sugar plantation in Jamaica which was managed by the Wedderburns, suggesting that exploitation of the slaves was a complex partnership business of money-making and forging new family connections. If Virginia was the focus of British slave grown tobacco, the West Indies was the focus of slave grown sugar and coffee and the Scots were in the West Indies in large numbers. By 1807 there were about 20,000 white people in Jamaica, about half of these were Scots and about one-third of the slave plantations were owned by Scots. British slaves were dressed mainly in Scottish linen.

At the end of slavery in 1834, the slave masters, who retained their land, were given free, so-called "Apprentice Scheme" slave labour for four years. Also, they were given over £2 billion (at today's value) by the British government to "free" their slaves (see page 54). The slaves were given nothing. The parasitic existence of the slave masters continued even after slavery was finally abolished in 1838, with the ending of the "Apprenticeship Scheme". After the abolition of Black slavery in 1838, the supply of British-made clothes and protein foods for slaves, such as linen clothes and slated fish respectively, declined suddenly. The ex-slaves in the Caribbean had no jobs or incomes to keep them alive and the inheritors of the benefits of British slavery showed no concern. The slavers pocketed the government's compensation of £20 million (1833-1834) for the loss of their human properties (slaves) and left their slaves to starve. Requests by ex-slaves in 1865 for fair consideration of their plight were dismissed with derision by the government of Queen Victoria and enlightened 'racists' such as Carlyle. This was the cause of the great loss of life in the Morant Bay Rebellion of Bogle and Gordon, in Jamaica, in 1865 which ended the neo-slavery of the decendants of slaves in Jamaica. Bogle, Gordon and many other Jamaicans were hanged. The power of the slave masters was removed finally when Jamaica and the other slave colonies became Crown Colonies, ruled directly from Britain. Slavery in Jamaica did not really end until the Morant Bay rebellion in 1865. Not one of the supportive voices from the anti-slavery movement was heard when Thomas Carlyle (1867) praised Governor Eyre for hanging Jamaicans that rebelled at Morant Bay in 1865. Carlyle berated black people as "Niggers" and "Quashes". He bemoaned the loss of the free labour which sustained British slavery... he and others could not accept that the parasitic "free meal" of British slavery was over. War-like rebellions were the only way black people could make the British government understand that slavery was wrong and, in time, would be unworkable.

In the greatest forced mass-transportation of people the world has known, about 20 million black Africans were transported, like animals, from the West Coast of Africa as slaves and about 10 million survived to work on the plantations. This transportation was part of a *Triangular Trade*. Slave ships sailed from British ports such as Bristol, Liverpool, London and sometimes Glasgow. On the West Coast of Africa slaves were packed onto the decks of ships, like sardines in a tin. These ships then sailed "the middle passage" across the Atlantic to the plantations of the New World. Voyages could last longer than a month. Sick or dead slaves were thrown overboard. Some slaves dismayed by this mysterious degradation fought to be free, others drowned themselves. Beatings were brutal...all this cruelty was within the laws of British Chattel slavery. Slaves were washed, greased and sold on arrival or sold-on to other destinations. Jamaica was not only a port for the sale of slaves; it was also a staging post for the distribution of slaves to other countries in the New World. Between 1700 and 1786, about 610, 000 slaves were transported to Jamaica. New slaves were subjected to "seasoning periods" of ill treatment, to condition them to work as dictated. The length of the daylight hours of the day determined the length of the working day of a slave. *The average working life of a slave was less than five years.* The third leg of the trade was from the slave colonies, back to Britain. The ships were laden with the produce of the plantations. A two-way trade also occurred. Ships sailed from Bristol, Liverpool, London, Glasgow, Greenock and Leith to the West Indies with supplies and white immigrants. They then returned to these ports with the produce of slavery.

The short working life of a Chattel slave mattered little to the slave owners. The slave trade made it easy to replace slaves. However, by abolition the slave islands were very well stocked with slaves. On the small island of Jamaica, there were, at the time, about 300,000 slaves. The slave masters had solid support in the British Parliament and in their local Assemblies because of their wealth. Without the vote, petitions helped to bring matters of concern to the Government. In addition to petitions and the great support from Quakers (1783) the members of the Society for the Abolition of the Slave Trade (1787) such as Granville Sharp, Thomas Clarkson, James Ramsay, William Dickson, Zachary Macaulay, James Stephen and Henry Broughton persuaded William Wilberforce to pursue the abolition campaign in Parliament.

Wilberforce's Parliamentary bill to abolish the slave trade was supported by a large number of petitions from Scotland and England but the bill was rejected at least seven times from 1791 before it passed into an Act in 1807. Black (non-white) activists such as Jamaican born, Robert Wedderburn (1762 - 1835) and African born Olaudah Equiano (1745 – 1797) also played an active part in securing abolition of the slave trade. Wedderburn was relentless in his attack on those who enslaved his family and his people in the West Indies. Robert Wedderburn's father, James Wedderburn, was a wealthy Scottish slave master who made his money in, Westmoreland, Jamaica. Robert's mother was a black slave, called Rosanna. James Wedderburn rejected his black son. The distinguished Professor and economist, Lord Bill

Wedderburn, QC, is a proud descendant of Robert Wedderburn. Bill Wedderburn earned his awards and is fiercely proud of his slave ancestor.

We are descended from great men like Robert Wedderburn and the leaders of our slave rebellions. It is baffling and difficult to explain that Scots like James Wedderburn and his family who suffered after losing the war at Culloden in 1745, could go to Jamaica and be so barbaric to black slaves in pursuit of money. Was it misplaced revenge, greed or the desire to recover what they had lost: pride, power and status? The evil mix of British slavery is complex and requires detailed study to unravel the diabolical nature of this event...an event, and its consequences, that still defy understanding. A small grant here and small grant there will not produce anything of scientific value. At its simplest, one may ask: *How could "enlightened people" allow Chattel slavery to go on for so long?* Those who think we should forget this slavery are under the illusion that we understand the potential of human beings to commit evil.

The abolition of the slave trade increased the price of slaves. Despite the efforts of the British Navy to stop the trade in slaves, slave traders still traded with Cuba and Brazil. American slavery did not end until 1865 and it continued to sell its surplus slaves. To counter the effects of the abolition of the slave trade, letters from slave masters (see page 65) often lamented the "waste" of feeding slaves incapable of doing profitable work and outlined that "breeding of slaves" was being tried to offset potential labour shortages that could occur because of the abolition of the British slave trade. Had British slavery been abolished totally in 1807, instead of 31 years later in 1838, the barbaric practice of trying to "breed" people would not have been enacted against black British slaves. Evil must be stopped with one debilitating blow or else it will grow again and spread as it did for 31 years after the abolition of the slave trade.

Religious and political justifications for slavery were provided by many people but probably the most devastating justification for the enslavement of black people came from respected philosopher David Hume in 1753. He stated, without reservation, that black people were inferior to white people...black people could imitate white people, not equal them. It is beyond belief that Hume, one of the great thinkers of the Enlightenment, could not see that differences in life-style did not reflect differences in intelligence. Because of his vast reputation as a thinker, Hume's bad reasoning was used by slave masters as scientific justification for the enslavement of black people. In Hume's time, slavery could not be criticised because of the power of the merchants...maybe Hume was concerned with his own self-interest when he contrived his racist conclusions. I was not far from Hume's Tomb in Edinburgh in 2009 when Barack Obama became President of the United States - the turning in Hume's grave was deafening!

Unfortunately, Hume's racist views are still at the root of racist thinking today. To have the British Parliament, rich merchants, political power and the whips and scorns of slave masters against you as a slave is beyond our comprehension. Yet, the slaves survived to be our ancestors. Through us, these slaves will live and their story will no longer be denied by mindless people, *as "a tale of bad history"*.

The British Parliament was reluctant to abolish the lucrative trade in human beings. Many MPs colluded for years to prolong slavery. A majority of Scottish MPs never voted for the abolition process. In May 1838, at one of the abolition votes, only 4 of 53 Scottish MPs voted for the abolition of slavery. Gibson-Craig of the Riccarton Estate, now the campus of Heriot Watt University, was one of these four men of justice. Abolition of the slave trade, before the abolition of total slavery, was the rotten compromise the abolitionists and Wilberforce accepted because of the intransigence of powerful government ministers such as, the Scot, Henry Dundas...rewarded later, with a very tall statue in St Andrews square in Edinburgh and the title of Lord Melville, for protecting British interests during slavery. He had family connections with the slave master, James Wedderburn. His political approach was simple. Slavery was awful but it was an essential part of the British economy and had to be prolonged. He knew that this cynical concept of self-interest could not be challenged in the short term. In the late 1700s and early 1800s, abolitionists such as William Dickson (a Scot) organised petitions against slavery. However, those who opposed slavery were out of step with the general view that slavery was in Britain's interest. Rev James Lapsley of Campsie in Scotland was so convinced of this that he ensured that those who opposed slavery were prosecuted. However, neither petitions nor prayer could have swayed Dundas away from his political plans for prolonging slavery for as long as possible.

Henry Dundas, Scotland's premier politician had informal names that reflected his power. One of these names was "Henry IX". He managed British slavery in the Caribbean with self-interest and patronage. For example, he promoted the careers of governors such as Alexander Lindsay, Lord Balcarres (1798) and Ninian Home (1792) on the British slave islands such as Jamaica and Grenada respectively. After a war with the Maroons in Jamaica, Balcarres exiled many of them to maintain the efficiency of slavery. Dundas protected and promoted the sugar, coffee, spice, cotton, thread and linen slave "business" of his countrymen. He did this with the might of the British Navy, votes from compliant members of parliament and money from the Bank of Scotland where he ruled as governor. The "business-activities" of Caribbean slavery changed Scotland from a poor to a rich country. Slave-grown fine cotton was worn by Scottish and English people. Scottish coarse linen was worn by slaves. Perth's development as a city was based to a large extent on providing linen clothes for British slaves in colonies such as Jamaica. On the 18th April 1797 the *Caledonian Mercury* newspaper in Scotland listed the number of slaves in the "British Sugar Colonies": 461, 684: 256,000 in Jamaica (1787); 62,000 in Barbados (1786); 37,808 in Antigua (1774) and 23,462 in St Kitts (1774)...these islands comprised the largest populations of slaves. The slave population in British Guiana (Guyana) was not listed because, although captured by the British from the Dutch in 1796 as Essequibo, Demerara and Berbice, these territories only became one British colony in 1814. In the *Caledonian Mercury* the total monetary value of 461,684 slaves was given as £38 billion (at today's value) with three exclamations marks of satisfaction. It is noteworthy that plantation land value, free labour, produce value and general economic value were not included in this figure of £38 billion. The *Caledonian Mercury* described British slaves as "property"...this was the Scotland and Britain of Henry Dundas.

William Pitt, the Prime Minister, although acknowledged as one of the most gifted of British politicians, was powerless, compared to Dundas, as regards the abolition of slavery. Pitt regarded his greatest failure, before he died in 1806, as not being able to abolish British slavery. At that time, Dundas was in charge of the British Navy and was also known as the uncrowned "king of Scotland". Like Napoleon, he tried to stop Toussaint L'Ouverture's slave rebellions in Haiti that led to Haiti's independence in 1804. He failed and many British servicemen died. However, at home, he made it clear to Wilberforce that the condition for Parliament passing the Slave Trade Act was...*delayed abolition of slavery*. Dundas's action triumphed and British slavery went on for another 31 years. Wilberforce and his abolitionist supporters accepted this rotten compromise. Granville Sharp and later Clarkson, both prominent members of the 1823 Society for the Mitigation and Gradual Abolition of Slavery throughout the British Dominions, regretted making this compromise but the power of Dundas, through Parliament, won the day, and the abolition of the slave trade was separated from the abolition of slavery. Indeed, thousands of slaves suffered and died during this bartered period of political delay. A delay which Elizabeth Heyrick, in 1824, found so unacceptable that she proposed courageously that British chattel slavery should be abolished immediately, not gradually as proposed initially by Henry Dundas (see page 129, 130, 131).

Mindful of the role of Henry Dundas in Scottish-Caribbean slavery it is strange that it has been proposed that 'freedom' on St Andrew's Day will be celebrated around the 41 metres high monument of Britain's uncrowned king of slavery.

The profits from slavery were so important to British interests that slavery was allowed to continue for another 27 years, after the abolition of the trade in 1807. After the abolition of slavery in 1834, there were another 4 years of delay, known as the iniquitous "Apprenticeship System" in which free slaves had to work for their old masters without a wage under a "milder" slavery. In this "milder" slavery, marriage would be allowed if sanctioned by the slave master. Women were to be flogged in private, instead of in public. Maximum lashes would be 39.

Percival (1762 - 1812) was a powerful politician during the abolition process. It is not often stated that he helped Wilberforce to secure the Slave Trade Abolition Act in 1807. It is not well known that he was assassinated by a disaffected merchant in Parliament...the only British Prime Minister to be assassinated. Another person that supported Wilberforce was John Newton, the converted slaveship captain who wrote the Hymns: *Amazing Grace* and *How Sweet the Name of Jesus Sounds*. In some ways John Newton's life (1725-1807) mirrored the ambiguity of the Church during slavery. Some Churches branded their slaves; others did not petition for abolition, others excluded slaves from worship while others were late in supporting the abolition process. However, it is important to mention that the fighting spirit of the slaves increased with Christianity, as the slave masters had feared. Therefore, before Samuel Sharpe was hanged in Jamaica, in 1832, for leading the Christmas rebellion, he made his position as a Christian clear. He declared that the only master he would serve was not the one that owned him on the plantations but the one that owned him in heaven.

The resolve of British slaves to help bring about the abolition of slavery is exemplified in the martyrdom of Samuel Sharpe in 1832. As regards the process of abolition, it is not well known that part of the power-struggle to end slavery was carried out by industrialists such as Samuel Whitbread II (1805), Thomas Buxton (1823) and Joseph Sturge (1836). Whitbread and Buxton were brewers. Their involvement in the abolition movement is interesting because it is unexpected. Brewers would have had very little interest in sugar as a brewing material because it was illegal, at that time, to use sugar to brew beer. Samuel Whitbread was leader of the Whig party and was head of the Whitbread family who were rich landowners and brewers.

Bearing in mind the political power of Henry Dundas up to 1805, it was astonishing that Dundas' political career was ended by Whitbread in 1806. Whitbread initiated the impeachment of Henry Dundas for mismanagement of Navy funds and although Dundas was cleared by his "friends" in the House of Lords his political career was over in 1806, one year before the slave trade was abolished. Turning from Whitbread to Buxton, in 1825 William Wilberforce passed the reigns of the abolition movement to Thomas Buxton. Buxton was a Member of Parliament and one of the abolitionists. He was a founder member in 1823 of the Society for the Mitigation and Gradual Abolition of Slavery.

Buxton was a rich brewer and was Master of Brewers' Hall in London in 1824. His mother was a Hanbury of the brewing company: Truman Hanbury and Buxton. His wife was Elizabeth Fry's sister and he helped to finance Fry's prison reform work. Elizabeth Fry's husband was a Fry of the Fry's chocolate empire. Many brewers were members of parliament and members of Brewers' Hall. Wilberforce's choice of Buxton may have been influenced not only by Buxton's commitment to social justice, it may have been influenced by Buxton's powerful industrial connections. To effect change goodness is not always enough. The ending of slavery had an economic base. The professed morality of abolishing the production of sugar by British slaves was diluted by the switch to importing cheaper slave-made sugar from Cuba and Brazil. Nevertheless, to bring British slavery to an end in 1838 rich industrlaists such as Joseph Struge helped to highlight the economic limitations of slavery in new industralised Britain.

Dr Johnson (1709-1784), the literary giant, described Jamaica as: a place of great wealth, a den of tyrants and dungeon of slaves. The Reverend William Knibb was an English Baptist minister. He arrived in Jamaica in 1823. On his arrival he said: 'I have reached the land of sin, disease (see page 128,130) and death'. He visited Scotland in 1833 to encourage the 53 to 55 Scottish members of parliament to vote to end slavery. However, Scottish MPs not only avoided the debates on abolition, they never voted in a majority to end British slavery...many did not bother to turn up to vote. Knibb was not well received in areas of Scotland which benefited significantly from British slavery in the Caribbean. He begged the Scottish people to help end slavery as follows: 'I plead for thousands of children of Scotsmen in slavery, children left by their parents...to the horrors of West Indian slavery'. This plea must have embarrassed the Stirling of Kier family because in 1749 James Stirling admitted that he had at least 23 children in Jamaica with slave women. Knibb's Memorial Church and High School are in Trelawny in Jamaica, they are now famous worldwide because Usain Bolt was a pupil at Knibb's High School.

To the slave master, politician and merchant, slavery was a "natural" pursuit of "self interest". The song, *Rule Britannia* was written by the Scot, James Thompson, in 1740. It puts so called European Enlightenment into its true context of shameful arrogance and interest in self that mocks: We enslave others, they don't enslave us. In addition, the great hypocrisy of British justice during slavery is summarised in the self-congratulating court cases of the British slaves, Somerset and Joseph Knight. Somerset was set free by Lord Mansfield in London in 1772. Joseph Knight was set free in Scotland in 1778.

These judgements made it clear that whilst slavery was not permitted in England and Scotland, it was permitted in the colonies of the West Indies where English and Scottish people ran rampant as slavers. This "two-faced" justice exemplified the kind of hypocrisy that kept the disease of slavery alive for so long and made it seem acceptable to white young men such as the poet Robert Burns (died 1796) who bought his ticket in 1786 to sail to Jamaica to become, in his own words, a "Negro driver". Thankfully, Burns did not sail. In his poem about "honest poverty", he wrote: *That man to man the world over/Shall brothers be...* However, the young white men that sailed to the West Indies became "Whippers-in" of slaves according to the poet Coleridge (died 1834). This was their way of achieving a large fortune quickly. Where was the brotherly love then? It certainly was not on the slave plantations. However, out of the evil of slavery has come, not only bad money but good things such as new nations of people, new pride in colour and self, new forms of music such as Blues, Jazz and popular music such as Rap and Reggae. The hymn *Amazing Grace* which was written by the ex-slaveship captain John Newton is also a legacy of slavery; so is *Ae Fond Kiss*, by Burns. He wrote it to bid his lady friend,

Clarinda (Mrs MacLehose) goodbye as she sailed from Greenock in 1791 to meet her husband who was a slave master in Jamaica. She informed Burns on her return to Scotland that her husband told her to return to Edinburgh alone because he was quite happy with his, *Ebony (slave) woman and mahogany children.*

Despite the constraints of a vicious slavery, the slaves fought for their freedom and the threat of a Haiti-type rebellion, where independence was granted by the French in 1804, was a constant worry to British politicians and slave masters. Over a period of one hundred years there was at least one dangerous slave rebellion in Jamaica every ten years in which both white slave masters and slaves died. Similar rebellions also occurred in other slave colonies. The maroons (black slaves of captured Spanish territories) were involved in some of these rebellions. In Jamaica they signed treaties with the British that freed them from working as slaves. The defiance and executions of great patriots such as Bussa (1816), Gladstone (1823) and Sharpe (1832) occurred after the abolition of the slave trade but sent a serious message to the British Parliament that total abolition would have to be given because the killings would not stop. As the Baptist Christian, Samuel Sharpe, said at his hanging in Jamaica in 1832: *I would rather die upon yonder gallows than live in slavery.*

The role of the British Navy in protecting British colonies from the French was expensive in life and money. Some British women signed petitions to abolish slavery because of the large numbers of sailors that were dying in the seemingly continuous battles with the French and Spanish. The industrial revolution in the 1830s was throwing up new problems of social unrest at home.

The control of Britain's slave business, 5,000 miles away, was also problematic. Sugar was cheap in Cuba and Britain wanted to "take advantage" of this source of slave-produced sugar. Despite British Naval patrols after the abolition of the slave trade, slaves were still being transported to Brazil and Cuba.

In general, mindful of the successful rebellion in Haiti by the slaves, British Chattel slavery was becoming dangerous, impractical and indecent. Full abolition was inevitable. The resistance of the slaves, against the most powerful country in the world, and their role in securing abolition should be given proper recognition. Many acts of slave defiance are mentioned among the terrible events recorded by the Jamaican slave master, Thistlewood, in his diary of 1750 to 1786. This diary is a dispassionate, personal catalogue of legal brutality and rape. In it, Thistlewood quotes a slave as saying: *If this is life then let me die.* This was a slavery that was worse than death. With a black lineage which started with Giants of black British rebellions such as Tacky, Sharpe, Bussa, Gladstone, Gordon and Bogle...why should I not fight to keep my black-slave identity. With such a defiant and distinguished history of survival why should I look elsewhere for an identity? As I said in one of my articles, my colour is me and nothing will change my position on identity. Each person has a right to choose his or her identity. In this regard, I am heartened that on Facebook that we, the Jamaican/Caribbean descendants of Larmonds, have come to refer to ourselves as Cousins and/or as the Clan Larmond. In terms of identity, no one has the right to tell people how they should refer to themselves by name.

The history of British slavery should be taught routinely so that people can make up their own minds regarding the contribution West Indian people have made to the development of Britain. Such knowledge will help to remove those areas of ignorance which produce racism.

The amount of money made from British West Indian slavery is impossible to estimate. A price cannot be put on suffering. Horace Walpole (1750), the British Member of Parliament, said that although Chattel slavery, *Chills one's blood*, the economy of Britain depended on the money made from this trade. Slave merchants and slave masters such as Scotsmen: John Gladstone (the father of William Gladstone, the British Prime Minister), Archibald Grant. James Ewing, William Cunninghame, Richard Oswald, George Bogle of Daldowie, James and John Stirling of Keir, James and Evan Baillie, William McDowall, Neil Malcolm of Poltalloch and James Wedderburn became multi-millionaires. For example, when John Gladstone died he left about £65 million (today's value). James Ewing's estate was worth about £22 million (today's value). English slavers such as, William Beckford and Henry Lascelle were even richer. William Beckford (1760-1844) owned 22,000 acres of slave plantations in Jamaica and was, at one time, the richest man in Europe...and one of the richest in the world. He was Lord Mayor of London and is reputed to have hired Mozart to give his son piano lessons. Money from slavery helped slave-owning families such as the Beckfords to buy their way into Parliament and into the aristocracy as stated elsewhere (see pages 50 and 51 with regard to the Wedderburns). In this regard, Beckford's son married Lady Margaret Gordon and his grand-daughter married the 10th Duke of Hamilton (1810). Slave owners and masters also built grand houses, schools and monuments, not in slave fields, but in various parts of Britain.

Powerful slave families such as the Lascelles and the Wedderburns had many slave plantations. The Lascelles had slave plantations in Barbados and Jamaica. They built, Harewood House in Yorkshire...one of the grandest stately homes in Britain. The present Lord Harewood is a Lascelle and has family links to the Royal Family through his late mother, HRH Princess Mary. James Wedderburn's father was hanged after the battle of Culloden of 1745. He and his brother went to Jamaica in 1746 and became slave masters.

The Wedderburn family of uncles and nephews built a "slave empire" in Westmoreland in Jamaica. The family eventually owned the following estates: Jerusalem, Retreat, Moreland, Paradise, Mount Edgecombe, Clenisia, Spring Garden, Baulk, Blue Castle and Blackheath. They also managed estates for absentee landlords such as Cunninghame who owned a 3,500 acre estate called Grandvale. After returning to Inveresk in Scotland in 1773 James Wedderburn bought a Lodge and married the daughter and heir of the last Lord Colville. His daughter (Joan) married Lord Selkirk who owned a substantial part of Manitoba (which included the Winnipeg area), Canada. One of his sons became Lord Advocate. Another son, Andrew Wedderburn-Colville, the one who stated that his black slave-born half-brother, Robert Wedderburn, did not count as family, managed his father's slave business in Jamaica while acting as Chairman of the West India Docks in London. He dropped the name Wedderburn and used Colville. He then became a Governor of the Hudson Bay Company and married Lord Auckland's daughter. Their son, Eden, also became a Governor of the Hudson Bay Company. Lord Auckland was a good friend of the Prime Minister, Lord Granville. Granville was Prime Minister when the slave trade was abolished in 1807. Andrew Wedderburn-Colville was the most powerful and celebrated Governor of the Hudson Bay Company and many places in Canada and the United States are named after him...as Colville.

I do not know how the black Jamaican descendants of James Wedderburn live in Jamaica but I am sure they are less well placed than his white descendants. They were not born with blood-stained silver spoons of slavery in their mouths. The present Lord Dundee is a descendant of James Wedderburn. In passing, James Wedderburn's brother's daughter, Louisa, married Lord Hope of Hopetoun...such were the benefits of British Chattel Slavery.

The brutal calculations by the sugar barons for the optimal operation of a sugar and rum producing estate such as the Wedderburns' Blue Castle estate in Westmoreland, Jamaica, would be that, 300 black slaves were required to produce 240 tons of sugar and 170 gallons of rum. *The Wedderburn style* of fruity aromatic rum is still produced in Jamaica today and is another legacy of Wedderburn slavery in Jamaica.

Although it can only be surmised how much money slave masters made from slavery in British colonies such as Jamaica, it is known that the British Government gave £20 million (over £2 billion at today's monetary value) to owners of slaves as Compensation for 'losing' their slaves when the slaves were Emancipated in 1833. This Compensation was shared between slave masters who owned thousands of slaves and British individuals who had acquired slaves as 'gifts' or had 'inherited' many, a few or even one slave as a legacy. Research work being carried out at London University by Draper shows that Compensation pervaded British society. Emancipation was the beginning of freedom for black people who had been enslaved for hundreds of years as chattel slaves...an inhuman business venture that has still not received the study it deserves. However, it is emerging that well known Scottish slave owners, who were also Members of Parliament, such as Ewing (Glasgow), Oswald (Ayrshire), Douglas (Dumfries), Baillie (Bristol), Dundas (Edinburgh), Ferguson (Banffshire) and Gladstone (Berwick on Tweed) received, at today's monetary value, millions of pounds Compensation for their slaves despite the wealth they had accumulated from the unpaid labours of their slaves. Many MPs did not vote for abolition because they owned slaves.

Sir Archibald Grant 1696-1778 embodied all aspects of the Caribbean slave master.   He was a Member of Parliament (MP) 1722-1732. The third of his four marriages was to the rich widow Elizabeth Callander, in 1751, in Jamaica. He acquired her estate and his son married her daughter. His fellow slave-owners, Sir Alexander Grant of Dalvey and Richard Oswald sold slaves from Bance Island near Sierra Leone (see page 37, Zachary Macaulay). Robert Burns, in his poem, Ode Sacred to the memory of Mrs. Oswald of Auchencruvie, attacked Mrs Oswald for enjoying an annuity of £10,000 per year from her deceased slave master husband, Richard Oswald...such was the wealth from British slavery and the social divisions it caused at the time. Sir Archibald owned the Monymusk rum factory and sugar cane plantation in Jamaica and was involved, like James Grant of Grant, in the production of linen, a cloth used to make clothes for slaves in the Caribbean. James Grant of Grant, who built Grantown-on-Spey, was a patron of Jamaican slavers who were from the Grant Clan. Sir Archibald returned home to Scotland, rich enough to build Archiestown, a town in the Highlands of Scotland. Stemming from his experience as a notorious slave plantation owner, he used his knowledge of sugar cane production to help develop Scottish agriculture. This development included the introduction of the turnip to Scotland! In terms of Scottish-Caribbean history during The Enlightenment, Archibald Grant, like other slave masters, was successful in benefitting himself and his country from British chattel slavery. He transferred the name Monymusk from his estate in Scotland to his slave plantation in Jamaica. As stated elsewhere in this book, the history of this slavery remains in many ways. Like the name Archiestown, the beneficiaries of slavery gave their names to roads, streets, lanes, places, schools and houses, in Scotland. These names include: Glassford, Ingram, Buchanan (see page 76), Ewing (see page 76), Oswald, Robertson's (Plantation), Speirs' (wharf), Baillie, Gladstone, Grant, Houston, Wedderburn, Stirling of Keir, Denniston, Dunlop and Dundas. Many of these men were Members of Parliament and were given Baronets, like John Gladstone or made Fellows of the Royal Society, like James Ewing. In passing, Jamaica Street in Glasgow was opened in 1763 to facilitate the business of trading with slave countries such as Jamaica.

In contrast to their masters, the slaves did not receive one penny Compensation. Indeed, the Apprenticeship scheme that was attached to Emancipation meant that the slaves had to (1833-1838) work 75% of their Emancipation time for their master without pay as an additional contribution to the £20 million Emancipation payment. Compensation payment per slave owned was made to the last shilling (s) and pence (d). For example and in contrast, James Campbell claimed £10, 725 19s 5d for 197 slaves; Louisa Ann Grant, £12, 765 13s 8d for 485 slaves; Charles Stirling, £6671 10s 3d for 321 slaves; Ann and James Dennistoun, £7298 16s 9d for 147 slaves; Colin Dunlop Donald, £1889 15s 5d for 89 slaves and William Gray, £230 for 4 slaves. This 75%-slavery continued for five years until British slavery was abolished totally in 1838. It is sad that the meanness of the politics of Emancipation dictated that the slaves, after hundreds of years of slavery, had to pay rich slave masters with their labour for being 25%-free from 1833 to 1838. In terms of unmitigated greed, it has been reported that John Gladstone was not happy with his share of Compensation money of about £11, 000,000, at today's monetary value. He reasoned that his slave estates in British Guiana and Jamaica were 'businesses' which could have earned him much more money, if the slaves had not been Emancipated in 1833. This was the man who started life as a humble grain trader in Leith, then he became a very rich slave owner, then a Member of Parliament, then the father of Cambridge educated William Gladstone, later Prime Minister, then a friend of Peel his Prime Minister, then a hereditary Knight and then the owner of the Fasque and Glen Dye estates with his own Church and graveyard in which in he was buried in 1851, leaving at least £65,000,000 at today's monetary value...a life very much unlike his chattel slaves who had slaved for him and provided his descendants with a comfortable future. In 2008, I became aware that Fasque House, not the estates, was sold and its contents alone fetched £2 million at auction at Christies. A small satin wood table, made in Jamaica in 1835, fetched £14,000...a pound in Jamaica today is worth $133 Jamaican dollars.

In 1833, the Earl of Airlie (the present Earl - see page 76 - presented me with an Honorary Doctorate degree at Abertay University in 2009) and the Earls of Hopetoun, Balcaress and Roselyn received financial Compensation for family owned slaves, as did Lord Colville of the Wedderburn Colville family. The Reverends Whyte, Forsyth and Skinner (Bishop of Aberdeen) also received financial Compensation for the loss of their slaves. Compensation was wide-spread across the country. Well known Scottish slave owners such as the Campbells, Douglases, Dennistouns, Stirlings, Dunlop Donalds, Hamiltons, Wedderburn-Colvilles, Robertson and the Bogles received many millions of pounds in Compensation for slaves. Bogle owned the Gilmorehill site on which Glasgow University found a permanent site. Bogle may also have owned the slave family that produced one of the National Heroes of Jamaica, Paul Bogle. The Scottish Bogles and their fellow slave-owing Scottish families and friends were some of the 'major recipients' of Compensation money in 1833. Many slave-owning families such as the Grants, Oswalds, Stirlings, Buchanans, Bogles, Dennistouns, Douglases and Dunlop Donalds intermarried and are related. In this way they kept their slave fortunes 'in the family fraternity of slavers'.

'Minor' recipients of Compensation who had acquired or inherited a few or even two or one slave 'cashed in' their human legacies after hearing the news that the government would pay them to forego their ownership of people they did not know. Recipients of Compensation who did not own slave plantations would have, in business agreements, be earning rent (Rentier) by letting their slaves. The addresses or locations of those who received Compensation are known. Many of the houses at these addresses still exist today. I have visited a few of them in Edinburgh. They are mostly in the New Town (northern) area of the city but addresses in Portobello and Mid Calder are given. Four of these addresses illustrate that the financial benefits of British slavery permeated British society at all levels. I know Forth Street well. I am President of the Edinburgh and Lothian Equality Council which is located at 14 Forth Street. Compensation for a few slaves was given to the resident of 24 Forth Street in 1833. The design of 24 Forth Street is different from any other house on the street. It has an iron balcony and railings of complex design and ornamentation. No 8 Queen Street has a grand neo-classical frontage and lavish internal design (see page 186). On the other 'poorer' southern side of the city, 13 Gilmore Place is one of three modest but large blocks of terraced houses. The original number 13, above the central door, is still visible. Number 1 Sylvan Place is a large granite stone built house of plain design.

Looking at the houses of 'minor' slave owners was as poignant as looking at the significant rewards of those who played a major role in British slavery, for example: Inveresk Lodge near Edinburgh... the home of the Wedderburns; the Gallery of Modern Art in Glasgow...the home of William Cunninghame before it become the Stirling Library; The Church that John Gladstone built in the extensive grounds of his estate at Fasque; the Stained Glass Window to the Oswald family in Glasgow Cathedral; the pink marble tomb of James Ewing in his Necropolis grave yard for the rich in Glasgow and the 42 metres' high statue to Henry Dundas (Lord Melville) in St Andrew Square, Edinburgh.

In the 18th century Glasgow was more important than London as regards trading in slave- grown tobacco and sugar. Glasgow had many Tobacco lords and Sugar barons. British slavery in America and the Caribbean made them millionaires. They helped to build the city of Glasgow. The family names of, Glassford, Ingram, Oswald and Buchanan/Spiers family were the names of Tobacco lords and, like the tobacco colony of Virginia and the sugar colony of Jamaica, all these businessmen of slavery had streets in Glasgow named after them. Towards the end of his life John Glassford's tobacco business declined. The Buchanans are a good example of 'business men' who changed from slave-grown tobacco to slave-grown sugar when historical events and falling profit necessitated a change in business strategy.

The Buchanan story did not start with tobacco. It started with the making of malt from barley. Ironically, the Buchanan narrative is of interest to me because I am descended from Jamaican slaves and my main research interest is in barley and malt and I am, at present, The Visitor (Head) of Glasgow's Incorporation of Maltmen...one of the fourteen Trade Incorporations that have been meeting in Glasgow for over 400 years. The Trade Incorporations started to meet in the Trades Hall on Glassford Street in 1794. Regarding Glassford Street, John Glassford bought Shawfield Mansion and estate in 1760. He died there until 1783. The decline of the Shawfield Mansion estate occurred after John Glassford's death and in 1793 Glassford Street was created and in 1794 the Robert Adam designed Trades Hall was built on Glassford Street. Previous to John Glassford's ownership of Shawfield Mansion in 1760, it was owned by Daniel Campbell, a Glasgow Member of Parliament who, in agreement with Article 13 of the Union, voted that the English malt tax should be imposed on Scotland. His house Shawfield Mansion was set on fire by Maltmen or supporters of the Maltmen or both in1725. Campbell used his financial compensation to buy the Island of Islay. In Scotland, the sale of malt preceded tobacco and sugar as a profitable business.

In 1694, George Buchanan was a maltster. He was also Visitor (Head) of the Incorporation of Maltmen. His son, George Buchanan in1719 was also a maltster and Visitor of the Incorporation of Maltmen. However, his son Andrew Buchanan (1725-1783), Provost of Glasgow, maintained and improved the family's fortunes by changing his trade from the making and selling of malt to the importing and selling of slave-grown tobacco. Buchanan Street in Glasgow is named after Andrew Buchanan. In fact, Buchanan Street was built on the old city centre land of the Buchanan family. The American Revolution (1775-1783) reduced the profits of Scots involved in the importing and selling of American slave-grown tobacco. Andrew Buchanan's son, George Buchanan (1758-1826) migrated to Jamaica and increased the family's fortunes by becoming a successful slave master, producing and selling sugar. As a result of this fortune, the family home of Mount Vernon was revived in 1802. The Buchanan family fortunes, derived from Jamaican sugar, allowed James Buchanan, of Glasgow and sometime of Jamaica, to donate £1 Million (at today's monetary value) to the Trades Hall of Glasgow for the education of children in 1857. It would have been helpful to Jamaican children if similar donations to education were made by slave master. However, despite their negative attitudes to the plight of their slaves on plantations in Jamaica these slave masters had positive attitudes regarding the legacies they left behind for their own people in Britain.

Less well-known slavers left money that changed their communities in Scotland. For example, Slave masters in Jamaica collected money to support Inverness Royal Academy founded in 1792. Captain John McNabb left money, earned from slavery, in 1802 which built the Dollar Academy in 1818. John Newland left money to build the Bathgate Academy in 1833. Robert Waugh, a joiner, made a significant fortune in Jamaica and built Harmony House in Melrose in the Borders region of Scotland in 1807. He became a friend of Sir Walter Scott and gave him financial help. In 1813 the Scottish town of Greenock housed one of the largest sugar businesses in the world. The grand, giant, warehouses that sit, in line, along the shore of Greenock are monuments to a slavery that was meant to last at least a thousand years. The wealth derived from slavery is of no great importance to me. However, what matters is that the countries that were devastated by this outrageous slavery require financial aid to help themselves overcome poverty derived from slavery.

Our heritage is not only related to our slave ancestors it is also linked to our surnames which were derived from slavery. Since they indicate a struggle of which I am proud, why should I give up or deny my lineage? For example, a glance at a Jamaican Telephone Directory shows that about 800 "English" Beckfords and about 2,300 "Scottish" Campbells are listed. This means that there are twice as many Campbells in Jamaica as there are in Edinburgh and surrounding areas. Indeed, there are probably more Campbells per square mile in Jamaica than there are in Scotland. This is not an anomaly. Similar distributions are found for many other English and Scottish names in the West Indies...confirming the long historical links which the West Indies have with Scotland and England. No matter what we feel about our British names...they tell us certain truths about our history and our heritage. Truth can be denied but it cannot be changed. A name does not make us what we are but who would be so ignorant of British -West Indian history to call us "outsiders" and tell us our ancestors played no part in building Britain? We are not recent incomers; we came into Britishness a long time ago when John Hawkins started the British slave trade in 1562 and Bermuda became the first recognised British colony in the West Indies in 1609. The Saltire cross of St Andrew of the British Flag dominates the flags of Scotland and Jamaica. It is not clear why this is so, but our histories and flags are linked and this will not change. We are here to stay.

Towards the end of slavery, British West Indian colonies were packed with slaves. For example, Jamaica's slave population in 1800 was about 300,000. America's slave population in 1800 was about 900,000. Jamaica is about 11,000 Square Kilometres in area: America is about 10,000,000 Square Kilometres in area. At the Emancipation of slavery in 1834, there were about 800,000 slaves in the British West Indies. The growth of this forced transfer of people, from one part of the world to another, against their will, has had a damaging effect on the economy and lives of the people of the West Indies. Notwithstanding, it is worth remembering that by 1800 the West Indies was by far the greatest money earning sector of the British Colonial Empire...contributing four-fifths of the earnings from the Empire. Despite the prejudices of people like Hume, black slaves manned an industry that was larger and more profitable than any operation in Britain at the time.

The soils of these slave lands are now depleted and cannot feed the people. Some people are asking for an apology for slavery. I would prefer grant aid to the West Indies rather than an apology...apologies are often not sincere and if sincere they are expected to remove responsibility. A small number of Churches in Scotland are funding a Jamaican Education Project. This is a good example of what the government should do for that part of the British Empire that gave so much and received so little. The descendants of British slaves that still live in the West Indies have earned the right to be given the help they need to remove the legacies of slavery that limit development.

The most effective help a developing country can have is help that reduces foreign exchange expenditure...this is the kind of help the countries that bled to build Britain during slavery require. That the contributions made by the ancestors of the black descendants of

British slavery to Britain are not acknowledged in education and that uninformed civil servants can be consulting on the validity of black identity, contribute to the factors which drive black youths to kill and dishonour each other. This kind of institutional racism wears a mask of mock concern that only fools the gullible. Instead of consulting on identity, why not consult on what is required to ensure that black, minority ethnic as well as deprived white people are provided with the education they need to access their rights in society.

If our children are taught in schools about the fortitude and dignity their black slave ancestors used to survive one of the worst crimes committed against humanity, their self worth would improve. In addition to this, the public need to be informed of how Chattel slavery sustained Britain for nearly 300 years before it was abolished. If this is not done before the end of 2007, the injustices of a long and cruel slavery will continue...and this commemoration will pass into another long period of uneasy silence.

To prevent this from happening, projects such as the one to erect a memorial to Mary Seacole (1805 to 1881), the Jamaican (British-Scottish) nursing heroine of the Crimean War, should be supported. Mary was born, Mary Grant, in Jamaica during British slavery. Her father was a Grant from Scotland. British (Scottish) history should honour this black (mixed race) heroine as it has honoured Florence Nightingale her contemporary for saving the lives of British soldiers at war. Fair history, equality and good race relations go together. In June 2016, I witness the unveiling of a statue to Mary Seacole in the grounds of St Thomas' Hospital in London; she looks unto the House of Commons.

During the commemoration of the ending of the slave trade we have heard long adulations to the abolitionists and the voices of those who are using Chattel slavery to promote "modern slavery". In contrast, the voices of the slaves have been drowned by all these voices of self-interest. The narrative of old Henry's slaves enlightenment (page 71) is an attempt to make us hear the small but significant voices of the slaves that lost their lives on British slave plantations in the West Indies.

Campbells in Jamaica

The Campbells in Jamaica began with the Scot, Colonel John Campbell. He came to Jamaica in 1700 after the financial failure of the Scottish colony of Darien, Panama.

Campbell David N
Campbell David P
Campbell David R
Campbell-Davis Sharon G
Campbell Dawn
Campbell Dawn 1
Campbell Dawn A
Campbell Dawn E
Campbell Dawn E
Campbell Dawnie
Campbell Dean E
Campbell Deanne T
Campbell Deanne T
Campbell Debbie
Campbell Debbieann M
Campbell Deborah A
Campbell Deborah D
Campbell Deita
Campbell Delceta
Campbell Delcita L
Campbell Delleta P
Campbell Delmore
Campbell Delores
Campbell Delores
Campbell Delores
Campbell Delores R
Campbell Delpharine
Campbell Delpharine P
Campbell Delrose
Campbell Delrose E
Campbell Delroy
Campbell Delroy
Campbell Delroy
Campbell Delroy

Campbell Dewitt
Campbell Dexter O
Campbell Dezerine
Campbell Diahann R
Campbell Dian A
Campbell Dian A
Campbell Diana E
Campbell Diana I
Campbell Diane S
Campbell Doanld G
Campbell-Dobbs Roxanne J
   Or
Campbell Dollis
Campbell Dolrol J
Campbell Donald
Campbell Donald
Campbell Donald
Campbell Donald
Campbell Donald
Campbell Donald C
Campbell Donald.K
Campbell Donald L
Campbell Donald M
Campbell Donald O
Campbell Donald S
Campbell Donna 236
Campbell Donna M
Campbell Donna M Mrs
Campbell Donna S
Campbell Donnath
Campbell Donovan
Campbell Donovan
Campbell Donovan
Campbell Donovan
Campbell Donovan F
Campbell Donovan K
Campbell Doran D
Campbell Doreen
Campbell Doreen

Campbell Elaine ....
Campbell Elaine ....
Campbell Elaine B ....
Campbell Elaine E Mrs
....
Campbell Elaine E Mrs
....
Or ....
Campbell Elaine L
....
Campbell Elaine R
....
Campbell Elaine V
....
Campbell Elescie L
....
Campbell Elese E
....
Campbell Elfreda ....
Campbell Elfreda A
....
Campbell Elfreda K
....
Campbell Elgay
....
Campbell Elin G ....
Campbell Elizabeth A
....
Campbell Ellette ....
Campbell-Elliott Lorna

RESIDENTIAL

Campbell Ethlyn M
....
Campbell Ethna H ....
Campbell Etta ....
Campbell Etta A
....
Campbell Eugena B
....
Campbell Eugenie ....
Campbell Eugenie
....
Campbell Eugenie
....
Campbell Eugenie Mrs
....
Campbell Eula D ....
Campbell Eulalee Mrs
....
Campbell Eulet N
....
Campbell Eulin ....
Campbell Euline V
....
Campbell Eunice ....
Campbell Eunice I
....

Campbell ..... aud ....
Campbell Elsie ....
Campbell Eltis C ....
Campbell Elveta V ....
Campbell Emize A ....
Campbell Ena ....
Campbell Ena M Mrs
....
Campbell Enid A ....
Campbell Enid C ....
Campbell Enid I ....
Campbell Enid L ....
Campbell Enid M ....
Campbell Enid M ....
Campbell Enid R ....
Campbell Enis W ....
Campbell Enith ....
Campbell Enthrose
....
Campbell Era-May
....
Or ....
Campbell Eric ....
Campbell Eric A ....
Campbell Eric G ....
Campbell Eric G
....

Campbell Evadne P ....
Campbell Evadney C
....
Campbell Evelyn ....
Campbell Evelyn ....
Campbell Evelyn
....
Campbell Evelyn ....
Campbell Evelyn A
....
Campbell Evelyn C
....
Or ....
Campbell Evelyn D ....
Campbell Evelyn J Mrs
....
Campbell Everald ....
Campbell Everton ....
Campbell Everton ....
Campbell Everton D
....
Campbell Everton E
....
Campbell Everton L ....
Campbell Evet M
....
Campbell Ewart ....
Campbell Ewen ....

A Letter Home To Britain From Slavery In Jamaica

William Adlam was the Supervisor of the Hermitage Slave Estate in St Elizabeth, Jamaica. This is one of the 'routine letters' he wrote home to, a John Weymss of Edinburgh, the Agent of the Moyes' estate and absentee slave owner who received Compensation money, after Emancipation (1833/1834), for his "rented slaves" (see page 56).

The year 1820 was 13 years after the abolition of the slave trade and 18 years before the abolition of slavery. It is clear that the abolition of the slave trade encouraged the development of the unbelievable practice of breeding people. However, whilst American slave population increased locally, British slave population declined because of resistance, malnutrition and brutal workload. This is the cruel consequence of applying half-measures in justice... In addition, those who are proud to be 'racist' should read this letter carefully and note the parasitic and barbaric sources of their diseased ideology. Adlam's letter exudes great greed, that is regarded by some as 'enlightened self interest'. However Bonthorn's request for his *'Mullato daughter'* is evidence that in the midst of the most terrible evil, nature's conscience will emerge to reaffirm our common humanity…

FROM MR ADLAM FEBRUARY 1st - 1820

Dear Sir,

I received your favors of the 29th Oct. and 27th Nov. and fully notice its contents, the supplies for the Hermitage by *Ann Grant* and *St Elizabeth*, also my supplies by *Ann Grant* are arrived and in good order and give satisfaction. The Mill and the Mill house that is required must be deffer'd for some time longer and I hope that the present crop will much better enable us to do it than the last. We shall not have finished crop before the latter end of March, if then, I mean the picking from the field, being rather weak handed we cannot go on as fast as I would wish, by the next packet I can better inform you nearly the number of casks we can make, if we have dry weather for some time to come – to pick in the remainder of the coffee that is in a manner nearly dry, on the trees, for want of strength to pick it when ripe on the trees.

I think we shall make a tolerable good crop, we are now using the old mill and I think will take off this crop without any and great expense, or indeed but triffling. I particularly notice your instruction in regard of the shipment of the crop in case it should prove an abundant one – That 10 or 15 tierces should be ship'd to London, or the one half to Glasgow and the other half to Bristol, which I shall attend to.

I think the twenty Casks sold at 96/ per Cwt = of # Coffee sold very low, and hope the coffee in Bristol will meet a better market the Ball containing 6 pieces oznaburgs* for me, the wrapper was much broke and the edge of one of the pieces of oznaburgs rather injured but not much. I think it would be better in future to send it in a Puncheon. As you mention you are particularly anxious to learn the probable extent of the crop this season on Hermitage. I have entertain'd for some time past my opinion that 100 Casks

* Coarse Scottish Linen made into clothes for slaves.

may be made, Mr McLean the Overseer thinks we make 80 Casks and no more, it depends on the weather being favourable in getting the remainder picked, you may partly know from this the extent of the Crop nearly – I have seen Capt. Wilson of the *Ann Grant*, he offered to take from 10 to 15 tons of Ebony at 1 guinea freight per Ton, after getting the Coffee picked in, I intend to set in to cut a few Tons for the *Ann Grant*.

Mr McLean received your letter date 17th Oct. last and my having wrote you an Account of the shirts and shoes disposed off, he thought it would not require any further answer from him to you immediately on the subject – since the receipt of your Letter I have not seen Mr Bonthorn concerning the purchase of his Mullatto Daughter, as we are weak handed on the Hermitage I should prefer his giving a well disposed Man or Woman to the property for her, than purchase her otherwise.

I once mentioned this circumstance to him, but he did not seem inclined to do it. It would be more for the advantage of the property, however I shall be guided by your advice hereon. I am very sorry to inform you we have a few days ago lost an old Invalid Woman named Nancy, she has been doing little or nothing for the property for some time past, and her loss is not much felt in consequence. The women on the Hermitage breed very slow indeed, which I cannot account for, and they are many of them good looking young women. I shall expect to hear from you by next Packet or the *Isabella* – I remain very respectfully

Dear Sir your most obed. Servt.

William Adlam

for articels sold belonging to you, I did not think it so
proper to bring it into the Hermitage Account with yours
The remainder of the things unsold, care shall be taken
to endeavour to dispose of them to the best advantage, the
Negroes on Hermitage have been and are now sickly, the
Docter left the property last week, and left nine very sick
in the Hothouse, chiefly with Fevers, from the North winds
setting in, which is rather unfortunate for us in time
of crop, however hope they will soon recover again & go
to their work, for every hand is now much wanted, I
shall be glad to hear from you again p.r the Ann Grant.
Mean time, I remain
            Dear Sir
                your most obed.t & humble Serv.t
                        William Adlam

                                     _____

From Mr. Adlam Feb.y 1.st 1820

Dear Sir I received your favors of the 24th Oct.r and
27th Nov and fully notice its contents, the supplies
for Hermitage by Ann Grant and St. Elizabeth,
also my supplies by Ann Grant are arrived and in good
order and give satisfaction. The Mill and Mill house
that is required shurt be defferd for some time longer
and I hope the present crop will much better enable
us to do it than the last, We shall not have finished
Crop before the latter end of March, if then, I mean the
picking from the field, being rather weak handed we
cannot go on as fast as I could wish, by the next packet
I can better inform you nearly the number of Casks we
can Make, if we have dry weather for some time to
come – to pick in the remainder of the Coffee that is in
a manner nearly dry, on the trees, for want of strength
to pick it when ripe on the Trees, I think we shall make
a tolerable good crop, we are now using the old Mill
and I think will take off this crop without any great
expence, or indeed but trifling, I particularly notice your
instructions in regard to the shipment of the crop in case
it should prove an abundant one – That 10 or 15
tierces should be ship'd to London, or the one half to
Glasgow and the other half to Bristol, which I shall
attend to, I think the twenty Casks sold at 96/ per Cwt –

of ⌂ Coffee sold very low, and hope the Coffee in Bristol will meet a better market – the Ball containing 6 pieces ornaburgs for me, the wrapper was much broke and the edge of one of the pieces of ornaburgs rather injured but not much, I think it would be better in future to send it in a Puncheon, As you mention you are particularly Anxious to learn the probable extent of the Crop this season on Hermitage, I have entertain'd for some time past my opinion that 100 Casks may be made, Mr McLean the overseer thinks we may make 80 Casks and no more, it depends on the weather being favorable in getting the remainder picked, you may partly know from this the extent of the Crop nearly – I have seen Capt. Wilson of the Ann Grant, he offer'd to take from 10 to 15 Tons of Ebony at 1 Guinea freight per Ton, after getting the Coffee picked in, I intend to set in to cut a few Tons for the Ann Grant. Mr McLean received your Letter dated 17 Octr. last and my having wrote you an Account of the Shirts and Shoes dispos'd of, he thought it would not require any farther answer from him to you immediately on the subject – since the receipt of your Letter I have not seen Mr Bronthom concerning the purchase of his Mulatto Daughter, as we are weak handed on the Hermitage I should prefer his giving a well disposed Man or Woman to the property for her, than purchase her otherwise – I once mentioned this circumstance to him, but he did not seem inclined to do it, It would be more for the advantage of the property, however I shall be guided by your advice hereon, I am sorry to inform you we have a few days ago lost an old Invalid Woman named Nancy, She has been doing little or nothing for the property for some time past, and her loss is not much felt in consequence, The Women on the Hermitage breed very slow indeed, which I cannot account for, and they are many of them good looking young Women, I shall expect to hear from you by next Packet or the Isabella — I remain very respectfully

Dear Sir Your most obed. servt.

William Adlam

Campbell Phyllis
29 Sundown Cres Kgn 10
Campbell Phyllis L Lloyds
Campbell Phyllis M
19 St Albans Ln Kgn 16
Campbell-Pinto J Content Gap Mvbk
Campbell Pixie V Esses Cnr MDay
Campbell Polly E
25 Hope Twn Rd Kgn 6
Campbell Princess Gabby St Mdvl
Campbell Princess A Green Pk BtHl
Campbell Quaverland
Lot 56 Marvins Pk Ocho
Campbell R 13 Central Av Kgn 10
Campbell R 26 Nautilus Av Kgn 17
Campbell R 12 Retreat Dr Kgn 17
Campbell R 3 Varma Rd Kgn 11
Campbell R A 123 Mahogany Dr SpTn
Campbell R G 22 Maureen Cres Ptmr
Campbell Rackiesha L
Apt 312 2a Washington Blvd
Campbell Racquel S
Lot 1 Pondside Rd Yala
Campbell Ralford E
16 Fletchers Dr MoBy
Campbell Ralph
23 Mansfield Wy Ocho
Campbell Ralston Thornton
Campbell Ralston A
1750 Carlisle Cres Cumberland
Campbell Raphael
45 Dolphin Sq Kgn 17
Campbell Raphael O
4 Zennia Av Kgn 11
Campbell Rarane O
Tnhse 21 2 Michigan Av
Campbell Ray 26b Allerdyce Dr Kgn 8
Campbell Ray Mammee Rvr Rd Kgn 7
Campbell Ray
19 Paddington Terr Kgn 6
Campbell Ray 10 Sandhurst Av Kgn 6
Or
Campbell Ray
5 Woodhaven Av Kgn 19
Campbell Ray Ltd
10 Sandhurst Av Kgn 6
Campbell Raymond
26b Allerdyce Dr Kgn 8
Campbell Raymond Venecia Ln Lnsd
Campbell Rebecca Nutshell Ewtn
Campbell Reclifton
Lot 249 Eltham Vw Brwk
Campbell Reece A Rev Union HpBy
Campbell Reginald O
6 Belvedere Cres RdHl
Campbell Reginald S
15 Friendship Pk Av Kgn 3
Campbell Rejeanne C
1a Belgrade Cl (19)
Campbell Renford E 6 Royal Av Ind
Campbell-Rennalls Ena M
41 King Av SpTn
Campbell Rennie Sunset Vill LaBy
Campbell Rhys D
1a Belgrade Cl Belgrade Mews Kgn 8
Campbell Riando G 25 Hope St Kgn 4
Campbell Ricardo
Lot 443 4e Greater Portmore Bra4
Campbell Richard A
41 Old Harbour Rd SJon
Campbell Richard E Barrett Twn
Campbell Richard E Shelly Rd Bamb
Campbell Richard E
Sigon Barrett Twn
Campbell Richard I
54 Gardenia Av Kgn 6
Campbell Richard S
Lot 93 Whitehouse Crds
Campbell Richard V
Lot 15 Ebony Dr Gnac
Campbell Rita E
Lot 1009 1st Seal Wy DkPn
Campbell Ritenella
4 Lancaster Rd Kgn 10
Campbell Robert 15 Elgin Rd Kgn 5
Campbell Robert A
Baptist Tutor Utcwi Golding Av Kgn 7
Campbell Robert C
Apt 206 Olivier Mews Kgn 8
Campbell Robert H
Lot 254 Old Harbour Villas OlHb
Campbell Robert M Strathbogie Svlm
Campbell Robert N Stettin AbTn
Campbell Robert R
193 Lorraine Dr MoBy
Campbell Rodlyn Back St Ocho
Campbell Rodrick B Thornton
Campbell Roger E
Lot 8 Austin Av MoBy
Campbell Rohan
21 1/2 Sewell Cres MyPn
Campbell Rohan S
Lot 112b Albion MoBy
Campbell Roland Archer Ln RdGd
Campbell Roland R
Lot 23 Hodges Hsng BkRv
Campbell Rollin O
112 Orange Bay Country Club OrBy
Campbell Rona V
Lot 142 Orangebay Country Club
Campbell Ronald Cessnock Kndl
Campbell Ronald
Lot 12 Phase 2 Seaview Gdns Kgn 11
Campbell Ronald
Lot 282 Sydenham Villas SpTn
Campbell Ronald G Ragsville GyHl
Campbell Roosevelt D
17 South Haven Yala
Campbell Rosa Basida Ln Lnsd
Campbell Rosa E
Lot 729 Catherine Hall MoBy
Campbell Rosalee Woolwich Lcva
Campbell Rosalie A
Lot 692 5th Wy Brae
Campbell Rosalyn 3a Long Ln Kgn 8
Campbell Rosalyn 81 Mars Dr Kgn 17
Campbell Rosalyn T
352 Mockingbird Circ OlHb
Campbell Rosamond
Lot 524 St Theresa Rd N E Gnac
Campbell Rose
Apt 18 1 Hillman Rd Kgn 8
Campbell Rose
96 Baldwin Cres Kgn 20
Campbell Rose Stewart Twn
Campbell Rose E 16 Canada Av Ducn
Campbell Rose E Richmond GsVy
Campbell Rosella E
Lot 1 Pitfour Hgts Grn1
Campbell Roselyn Jackson Twn
Campbell Rosemaria A
Walderston Miz2
Campbell Rosemarie
Lot 72 Fern Clavers Grn1
Campbell Rosemarie E
1 Sunshine Villa Kgn 8
Campbell Rosenell E
33 Princess St Flmo
Campbell Rosevelt
Lot 6 Pimento Dr Rbno
Campbell Rosevelt 6 Pimento Dr Rbno
Campbell Roslyn 27 Bascayne Dr Ptmr
Campbell Rowan Hopewell Hhgt
Campbell Rowan G
Lot 56 Grant Av SpTn
Campbell Rowena L
Lot 122 Pitfour Grn1
Campbell Rox-Ann A Sweden St GsVy
Campbell Roy Coakley LrTv
Campbell Roy Lillyfield Bamb
Campbell Roy Tulsa Rd KnPk
Campbell Roy C Flagaman TrBh
Campbell Roy L Lot 10 Kingsland SpTr
Campbell Roy L Round Hill MyPn
Campbell Roy M Hyde CkTn
Campbell Roy S 1 Eberle Dr Ptmr
Campbell Roy W Siagon BtWn
Campbell Royan C
32 Riverview Est Yala
Campbell Royland White Horses PsPn
Campbell Rubertha C
Scarlett Hall Flmo
Campbell Ruby 24 Ashbury Av Kgn 3
Campbell Ruby Greenvale Mdvl
Campbell Ruby
Lot 490 7w Greater Portmore Brae
Campbell Ruby
Suite S205 6-12 Newport Blvd
Kgn 13
Campbell Ruby
6-12 Newport Blvd Suite S205 N P W
Campbell Ruby M 29 Delido Dr SpT1
Campbell Ruby M 34 Ocala Wy Wldn
Campbell Rudolph A
3 Ceiba Cres Kgn 11
Campbell Runcey D
Institution Dr StCz
Campbell Rupert Calabash Bay TrBh
Campbell Rupert 3 Pamela Dr Kgn 20
Campbell Rupert
16 Toronto Cl Kgn 10
Campbell Rupert R
Barneyside Westmorland
Campbell Rupert S
587-N Kelly Pl Ptmr
Campbell-Rushton Kerri-Gaye A
17 Barrington Dr Kgn 19
Campbell Ruth
Lot 108 3e Greater Portmore Brae
Campbell Ruth E Mrs
9 Bayview Cl Wik3
Campbell Ruth L Wakefield Lnsd
Lot 879 Westgreen MoBy
Campbell Ryland G Kingswood Svlm
Campbell Ryland S
Lot 188 Hills Borough Terr RoHl
Campbell Ryland T
5 Farringdon Hgts Kgn 6
Campbell S 8 Newton St Flmo
Campbell S 44 Westminster Rd Kgn 10
Campbell S A 6 McLaughlin Dr Kgn 3
Campbell S M
Lot 204 6w Greater Portmore Brae
Campbell S R M
17/1 Fern Grove Ocho
Campbell Sadie 3739 Adair Dr Ptmr
Campbell Samuel 6 Eustace Pl Kgn 10
Campbell Samuel
120 1/2 Mtn Vw Av Kgn 3
Campbell Samuel A Trinity Prus
Campbell Samuel M Dover WrCs
Campbell Sandra Howells Con MyPn
Campbell Sandra
Lot 4 Rosemount MoBy
Campbell Sandra
T 78 Quads Nurses Residence Kgn 7
Campbell Sandra
49 White Hall Av Kgn 8
Campbell Sandra A 9 Miles BlBy
Campbell Sandra E
Lot 151 Rosemount Hsng MoBy
Campbell Sandra K
Lot 49 2w Greater Portmore Bra4
Campbell Sandra M
26 Bolivar Av Kgn 20
Campbell Sandra R
Burnside Valley Rdt1
Campbell Sandria Top Geneva GrHl
Campbell Sandria A 209 Zell Av Ptmr
Campbell Santata Cauldwell
Campbell Sarah M
Copperwood Dr Luce
Campbell Satira P
35 C Burbank Av Kgn 19
Campbell Scarlett A
29 Cosmos Cres Kgn 20
Campbell-Scarlett Susan E
2-6 Birdsucker Dr Kgn 8
Campbell Seaford
Sangsters Hgts Chtn
Campbell Seaton A
8d Albert St Kgn 16
Campbell Sekayi 8 Denham Av Kgn 19
Campbell Selina A
34 Deanery Av Kgn 3
Campbell Selma
164 Olympic Wy Kgn 11
Campbell Selvin Lot 7 Galina Av Glna
Campbell Sephlin N
Lot 145 Gt Hse Dr Ducn
Campbell Sereta A
4 Lyndford Av Kgn 10
Campbell Serryrona
Race Course Tollgate
Campbell Shana 38 Westbury Cr Ptmr
Campbell Shane M Lampard Frnk
Campbell Sharmaine N
Tremolesworth Highgate
Campbell Sharman M Mrs
32 Middlesex Av Ptmr
Campbell Sharon
10 Davidson Cres Kgn 20
Campbell Sharon Lot 274 Upr Ft Hlsh
Campbell Sharon
25 Tavern Cres Kgn 6
Campbell Sharon Tryall Hgts SpTn
Campbell Sharon B
28 Longford Rd Kgn 3
Campbell Sharon C
Apt 6 5c North Av Kgn 10
Campbell Sharon C
7 Bonitto Vale Mdvl
Campbell Sharon C
3 Chatsworth Av Kgn 11
Campbell Sharon C
10 Marlowe Av Kgn 20
Campbell Sharon D Kingsland Hatf
Campbell Sharon F
Lot 211 Norwood Gdns MoBy
Campbell Sharon I
Apt E5 Skycastles Columbus Hgts
Campbell Sharon I
376 Jimbling Pl Ptmr
Campbell Sharon J
17 Bay Farm Rd Kgn 11
Campbell Sharon M Coffee Piece Clon
Campbell Sharon M
100d Maxfield Av Kgn 13
Campbell Sharon M
Lot 481 3 West Greater Portmore
Brae
Campbell Sharon N
Middlesex Benbow
Lot 411 4e Greater Portmore Brae
Campbell Sharon P
228 Ventura Rd Ptmr
Campbell Sharon V
2e Glasspole Av Kgn 2
Campbell Shaun O
113 Mtn Vw Av Kgn 3
Campbell Shaunette
Big Yard Kings Vale
Campbell Shawn A 330 Archid Cl
Campbell Shawn A
6 St Johns Rd SpTn
Campbell Sheila
1 Badminton Terr Mdvl
Campbell Sheila A
1a Clarks Twn Mdvl
Campbell Shelaine
925 Dominca Cres C MoBy
Campbell Sheldon J
Lot 960 Willowdene Thru-Wy SJon
Campbell Shelley D
9 Mayfield Dr Kgn 19
Campbell Shelly-Ann A
91 Annandale Av Kgn 20
Campbell Sherece E 9 Brooks St OlH
Campbell Sheree E
11 Sheriton Pk Cres Kgn 10
Campbell Sherill L Granville
Campbell Sherine
25 Ashoka Rd Kgn 11
Campbell Sherine C
Lot 110 8w Greater Portmore Bra4
Or
Campbell Sherline Canaan Dumf
Campbell Sherman A
13 A Charlton Av Kgn 6
Campbell Sherna A
Lot 34b Grange Pen Liliput RoHl
Campbell Shernette S 65 8 West
Campbell Sherril H Mrs
20 Lynmar Dr Mdvl
Campbell Sherryl A 110 Capri Cl MrP
Campbell Shirley Alexandeia
Campbell Shirley Marlborough Rcmd
Campbell Shirley
2 Richmond Hill PtAn
Campbell Shirley
20 Windsor Av Kgn 5
Campbell Siddean G
Lot 288 Seville Hghts SABy
Campbell Sidney A 42 Reef Av Kgn 1
Campbell Silbert O Duncans
Campbell Simon B
3 Walcott Av Kgn 20
Campbell Simone 29 Portsmouth Av
Campbell Simone E Trinity PtMa
Campbell Simone K Charles Twn
Campbell Simone N
33 East Palm Av PtAn
Campbell-Smith Andrea
6 Dahlia Av Kgn 11
Campbell-Smith Cordelia S
Mt Ogle TlHl
Campbell-Smith Janinne
157 Cyprus Dr
Campbell-Smith Mary L
Bliss Pasture Wkfd
Campbell Sonia Chapleton Cht1
Campbell Sonia
Lot 19 Orange Rvr Rcmd
Campbell Sonia 10 Wesley Cres BrTn
Campbell Sonia A Main St Spld
Campbell Sonia C White Rvr Ocho
Campbell Sonia E Danvers Pen
Campbell Sonia G
Lot 381 7e Greater Portmore Bra4
Campbell Sonia M
Lot 850 Sapphire Av Brwk
Campbell Sonia M
Lot 423 3e Greater Portmore Brae
Campbell Sonia V
Lot 79 Cornwall Gdns MoBy
Campbell Sophia
22 Hathaway Dr Kgn 19
Campbell Sophia J
45 C Waltham Pk Rd
Campbell Sophia L
2 Dolphin Sq Kgn 17
Campbell Sophia L 27 East Rd Kgn 1
Campbell Sophia P
157 Miranda Cl Ptmr
Campbell Sparton A Station Rd LtLn
Campbell Spencer C 20 Dade Dr Ptm
Campbell Spencer N
18a Pretoria Rd Kgn 13
Campbell St Claver Bounty Hall
Campbell St George
1 Terra Cotta Cl Kgn 8
Campbell Stacey A
Faith Ln Canoe Pond Ocba
Campbell Stacey A
11 Hampton Dr SpTn

Slave's Enlightenment

The different voices of the narrator are English, Ebo, Yoruba and Jamaican patois.

In a solemn and dignified voice, old West Indian Henry said to us: "Be still and listen...

We were caught, bought, shipped and enslaved
Found hope in God's grace and were saved...
So, why were we not as good as you?

You forced your culture on us in short time
But destroying ours was the greater crime
This dishonouring was long and brutally done
And has made us all what we have become...

So, why were we not as good as you?
During our slavery we had many fears
That your legal codes would kill us
And damage our children for years...
So, why were we not as good as you?
Nyaa, ọ gini bọ na anyi adiro nma ka unu?
Kilode ti awa ko se da to eyin?
Soe, wa mek unu tink unu betta dan we?

You destroyed our families and gave us one name:

Nigger, Quashi
Sambo, Boy
Horatio, Wallace
Sarah, Jane...
Nyaa, o gini bo na anyi adiro nma ka unu?

You derided our music which was "noise" to your ear
But it gave us a voice that has lasted for years.
You sneered at our colour and laughed at our frame
But we had your children since our blood is the same...
Soe, wa mek unu tink unu betta dan we?

You preached we were 'subhuman but pleasing'
Which Hume and Carlyle confirmed with "reasoning"
But they would not have been clever then
Had they been taught in plantation pens
Soe, wa mek unu tink unu betta dan we?

No writer, preacher, politician of worth
Should have been silent for so long
When kith and kin inflicted such hurt...
Kilode ti awa ko se da to eyin?

Our beaten bodies were sore with pain
Yet you branded and bred us and sold us for gain...
Kilode ti awa ko se da to eyin?

We dug strange fields in New World's dew
And were oft-times sick un-noticed by you
We tried our obeah but it failed
To protect us from the evil that prevailed...
Nyaa, ọ gini bọ na anyi adiro nma ka unu?

What was our price, what was our worth?
To live in a hell you created on earth
You ate or sold the food we grew
And our children died instead of you...
Nyaa, ọ gini bọ na anyi adiro nma ka unu?

Our dead children brought great sorrow
But our steely women were our tomorrow
They were the metal of our arm and eye
That drove us daily to defy...
So, why were we not as good as you?

When we fought and rebelled in our defence
You hanged or slow-burned us for impudence
Often in dark silence we would cry
If this is life, then let us die
And fly from the self interest of the lie...
Kilode ti awa ko se da to eyin?

We ate scraps and lived like rats to survive
But fought and "smiled" to remain alive

We are the "savages" that made you rich
But you buried us in a dirty ditch...
Nyaa, ọ gini bọ na anyi adiro nma ka unu?

You whipped our faces, put filth in our mouths
Which you tied shut, to prevent spitting out.
We endured this "civilised" violence alone
Where your prosperity and prejudices were sown
Only hypocrites and cowards deny their past
Because, good or bad done is meant to last...
Soe, wa mek unu tink unu betta dan we?

Our slavery was a dream rape
From which there was no escape
It was a nightmare come true
A world away and chained by you
The enlightened and the brave
That, "never, never will be slaves"...
So, why were we not as good as you?

Chained, we heard the 12th of April's cannons groan
The hundred year's dice of war was thrown
Again and again we were the prize
In a game of greed you had devised...
Kilode ti awa ko se da to eyin?

Unlike the progenies of animal and grass
Our children will remember the past

But no task on earth is harder
Than to redress the "sins of the Father".
Abolition was not an Act divine,
It was then politic to cover the crime...
Nyaa, ọ gini bọ na anyi adiro nma ka unu?

From masks of mock enlightenment,
devious people will say:
Others suffered in a similar way
But such denial and cultural play
Will not wash this cruel crime away...
Soe, wa mek unu tink unu betta dan we?

We were not chattel to slave and kill
We have the same humanity:
Love, rage and will...
So, why were we not as good as you?"

For surviving the most profitable evil the world has known
Put up no stone...just repair the damage done, alone.
Our right to be black and live here is not for review...
We paid a bitter price to live like you.

GHP

Musical reference to emancipation and abolition:
see, myspace – susie palmer music

The neo-classical marble busts on either side of me are of slave owners James Ewing and James Buchanan, in the Merchants' Hall of Glasgow.

Lord Airlie, whose ancestors were slave owners, presenting me with an Honorary Doctorate in Science at the University of Abertay, Dundee.

Preface To Britishness

PREFACE

The time of The Enlightenment Abolished gave us the 'reason' of Hume and Rousseau and the racism of New World slavery. Racism is cruel and is the creed of irrational and ignorant people who wrongly believe that skin colour confers superiority. In this regard, many people, whose lives are historically mixed with Britishness, are denied a rightful place in British society because their skin colour is not white. The original concept of Britishness was not about skin colour, it was about a family of different people who shared a political history that emanated from Britain...the rights of these people cannot be changed by racist rhetoric or any other form of nonsense, designed to dishonour black people.

Failure to overcome social racism may indicate that our approaches are incorrect. In order to make meaningful progress, we need to find ways to convert the racists instead of continuing to preach, to small purpose, to the converted. Our racism is not only a cruel legacy of New World slavery: racism is a lie that kills...

The Enlightenment Abolished is neither a history, nor a poem, nor a comment on the pain of the disadvantaged. *The Enlightenment Abolished* is merely a glimpse of one evil event in history...*our slavery*. A large number of people are not aware of the terrible role that their ancestors played in New World slavery. And, although slavery is an important part of their history, it has never been acknowledged or taught. Such neglect tends to support the view that an evil ignored in education is often an event no one wishes to remember. This book is a short narrative of events in the life of a Jamaican immigrant who came to the Mother Country as a boy and believes that New World slavery influences the way we live today and is an essential feature of Britishness. In many ways, our slavery is comparable to other human evils but its cruelty went beyond civilised understanding. This reflection is in the form of a dream. In this dream there are no recommendations for either reparation or revenge…it is a celebration of survival. I have dreamt this dream since I was a carefree child, playing cricket in Race Course in Kingston, Jamaica, on dusty stony ground.

Race Course was a rugged, dangerous and circular waste land in central Kingston where children played and fought and where adults walked during the day and courted and watched cycle racing on Friday nights. Race Course was dusty in the dry season but in the wet season it was covered with a plant that crept along the ground. We called it police macca because, its yellow buttercup-like flower produced a small round fruit covered with thorns which 'arrested' movement when lodged in the soles of our bare feet. One of my weekly jobs in the house was to collect police macca runners which were used to make bush tea for breakfast. Like many other children, I roamed the streets of Kingston, barefooted and without a care. This happened every day except Sundays... on Sundays, I followed my Aunts to Church. Sunday was God's day in Jamaica, that beautiful island of wood and water where slavery was 'legal', long and brutal.

Slavery not only gave us our British way of life, it also gave us our Church that was very large and its walls were deep and solid. The bricks, oak benches, tiles, fittings and a framed poster of Scottish Achievers came from Britain over a period of nearly 170 years. The framed poster was made in a place called Kirkcaldy, in Scotland.

My family always sat on the same bench…it was unofficially the Larmond's bench and no one else ever sat there. The pulpit was high up near the organ and the choir, and when the organ broke from old age and overuse, a man came from Britain and made it play again.

Reverend Nichol started my dream. He was sent to us from Britain to be the Minister of our Church. Our Ministers always came from Britain. He was a kindly man. His hair was auburn-brown and my Aunts said that he was as nice looking as King George. His wife had sky blue eyes and wore long floral dresses. When I was at primary school, she gave us buns and powdered milk after the 1951 *Hurricane*. The powdered milk made us sick for a long time. Reverend, as we used to call him, constantly asked us to give our lives to Christ and because we all loved him, we did so nearly every Sunday…but especially on Decision Sunday. He gave me a Sunday school prize once for *Regular Attendance*. However, I had very little input into this attainment. My Aunts' view on Church attendance was simple. If you cannot go to Church, you must be sick and if you are sick then you must take a large dose of castor oil! My Sunday diet of Church attendance was as follows: Morning Service, Sunday School, followed by Night Service. The Church was never silent and its clear voice reassured us…it was our education.

Reverend was the only person we knew who had a car and he took me to the doctor when I was too sick to be cared for by my Aunts. Most of them worked as domestic servants in St Andrews, the then colonial part of town, and could not afford to pay. I was concerned for him because all the Ministers that came to us from

Britain died of the fever. When he died we gave him a glorious funeral. I can still hear the metal shoes of the black, black-plumed horses slipping on the wet, worn tramlines, as his funeral carriage turned from Princess Street into North Street. He did not want to be taken back to Britain so we buried him in the Churchyard. Every Sunday, after Sunday school, I used to sit on the cool marble of his tombstone and watch people pass and trams trundle by. In season, the large red flowers of the Royal Poinciana would shed their golden pollen on his grave. We called this grand tree the cassha tree because of the noise its long, dry fruit pod made when shaken in fun or in playful fights.

I often remember the Reverend at Christmas Service preaching in the breaking light of the day. My Aunts would wake me at 5 a.m. and we dressed ourselves, in our *Sunday-best*, for Church in the fluttering light of the oil lamp and walked, in silence, the long distance to Church. At East Street we passed the ghostly old colonial house, with its large twin stairs and high garden walls. The service was held earlier than usual so that the children could go downtown to Christmas Market at Queen Victoria's Park. There were other services that I remember: There was the solemnity and calmness of our Three Hours Service on Good Friday with my Aunts propping me up as I fell asleep. There were the flickering magical candles of Candle Light Service; the aromatic smells of the fresh fruits and bread of Harvest Service and the noisy Friday Morning Services when all the school children gathered in the Church for a bit of pushing and shoving but mostly for praying and singing. Reverend Nichol will always be at the centre of these kind and gentle memories.

The activities of Mr Chen's corner shop reflected some of the special events of the Church. He sold raisin-filled buns and Cheddar cheese at Easter, specially moulded breads at Harvest and large rum-raisin cakes at Christmas. Among other things, he sold Cadbury's milk chocolate, Kellogg's corn flakes, potato crisps, Libby's tropical fruit salad, Camp coffee, Fry's cocoa, Lipton's tea, hot peppery patties (spicy descendents of the Scottish bridie) and Tate and Lyle's white granulated sugar, which were 'exported' from Britain. I used to add this list of expensive 'ethnic' food products to my requests from God in my daily prayers, but they never materialised while I was in Jamaica! However, sometimes my Aunts would weaken and buy treats such as wet-salted pig's tail and dry-salted codfish (saltfish), which also came from Britain.

The salted pig's tail was made into a stew which we ate with yams or boiled rice. The salt fish was cooked with akee (ackee) and eaten with boiled or roasted breadfruit. Both these plants were brought to the island, in 1778 and 1793 by Admiral Rodney and by Captain Bligh respectively to feed black people that were described by our teachers as…'the slaves'. Reverend told us that Jamaica was discovered by Columbus in 1494 but had been part of the British Empire since 1655, long before the creation of the Union of Great Britain, and that Britain was the *Mother Country* embodying and respecting diversity in a family of different cultures. Jamaica won its independence in 1962 but many important ties remain, with regard to our religion, language, education, laws and black and white ancestry.

Throughout its long history, Jamaica has been poor, proud, and defiant against injustice (as at the Morant Bay Rebellion in 1865).

The two Jamaican heroes of this rebellion were Paul Bogle and George Gordon. Their Scottish surnames relate to the slave heritage of these great men whose Britishness made them realise that rights denied required personal sacrifice to be achieved. Therefore, as free men, they fought for the right to live with dignity, just as the Tolpuddle Martyrs had done in England a few years before in 1834, one year after slavery was abolished. The Tolpuddle Martyrs were transported…but Jamaican Martyrs, Bogle and Gordon (1865) and Samuel Sharpe (1832) were hanged. The terrible torture that Jamaicans suffered during and after slavery never grew into disloyalty. They fought for the Empire when called and, as a boy, I remember the warm welcome we gave Winston Churchill. The welcome was as warm as a tropical summer's day and equal to the welcome we gave to Haile Selassie. Churchill sat on the back seat of a big black car with the Governor, Sir Hugh Foot, the brother of Michael Foot, a past leader of the Labour party. Churchill smoked a large Jamaican cigar and waved two fingers in the sign of a 'V'. I did not know what this meant but we waved our Union Jacks for him as we did for the Queen when she was crowned in 1952.

Jamaica is one of the best known islands in the world and has been given a degree of attention that compares only to the unfair size of the poverty that it now endures. To many, the perception is that Jamaica is that musical place, associated with drugs and violence. This is a small and lopsided view of a country that has contributed more wealth to the world than it will ever receive, while enduring a most pernicious slavery for hundreds of years. A deprivation that it now bears alone. Like the majority of any society, most Jamaicans are against crime and, by world standards, the comparatively small but unacceptable transport of drugs into Britain from Jamaica has damaged a long historical relationship, causing a British visa system to be imposed on the island in 2003.

The majority that obey the law should not be made to suffer because of the illegal folly of the few. That we who slaved for Britain without pay should now have to fill in visa forms and take citizen tests, is to us 'the worst of sins'.

Reverend Nichol believed that reading was better than writing and arithmetic because reading enabled us to read the Bible. He also believed in what he called British order and contentment, so he made us form long queues round the Church and the School, and with vigorous conducting, taught us to sing songs in rounds, such as: 'Rule Britannia' (that strangely boastful song, written by the Scot, James Thomson during slavery), 'Row Boys Row', 'O, my love's like a red, red rose', written by the great Scottish poet, Robert Burns, who applied to be a slave master in Jamaica), 'Who is Sylvia', 'Loch Lomond', 'Where the bee sucks', 'I'll Be A Sunbeam For Jesus', 'Amazing Grace' (that popular hymn written by John Newton an ex-slaver), and many others, including, 'Eternal Father, Strong To Save'. The latter song was usually sung for people who were emigrating to 'better themselves' in America or Britain. They sang it for my Mother and her cousin, in 1948, when I was eight and for me on the Sunday before I left for London to find a job to help my Mother. I was fourteen years old. My father went to America to pick oranges in 'farm working' when I was six years old but we never heard from him and according to my Aunts, "God provides for you so *He* is your Father." However, when my father died in New York thirty seven years later, my Aunts and my Mother were content that I went to Harlem to bury him.

As a child in Jamaica, 'bettering oneself' also meant attending a private secondary school and taking examinations such as, Cambridge School Certificate or Scottish Matriculation and Highers. These were controlled by Examination Boards in England and in Scotland, respectively. This route to 'betterment' required money that was beyond the means and possibilities of most of us. Therefore, we took our shiny blue-black British Passports and, with British 'on your bike' initiative, boarded expensive British Cunard line boats and B.O.A.C. planes and travelled to find work in the Eldorado of our dreams…*the Mother Country.*

My Mother was my Mother but my Aunts mothered me, especially my cousin Liz's mother. Her name was Aunt Agatha but I called her Mama Gatha. She often intervened when punishment sessions became extensive and smiled as she helped me to read the Bible. My mother sailed from Jamaica on the *Mauritania* on a clear, but windy day. The brown baby seagulls whistled for food and the humming birds dallied in the breeze. Important losses that we cannot change must be coped with and endured.

The snow sparkled like jewels in the night-light when she arrived in London. No-one would rent her a room, so the Salvation Army took her in. She worked hard in menial jobs, lived on very little, and never took a holiday. My Grandaunt and my Aunts looked after all the children in the family. The small amount of money my Mother sent to them from Britain helped to feed my brother and me. Her postal orders always came in blue Air-letters which gave up their contents of money only after being torn to bits! My Aunts were my Mother's eight sisters – she was the youngest. My Mother also had an elder brother, uncle Ferdy. I met him for the first time when he returned from Panama. He was a labourer on the Panama Canal. He had many gold teeth and dressed neatly. His clothes smelt of moth balls. There was a 'bosi' air about him... he knew the ways of the world and we did not...

My Grandaunt would not let him live in the house so he lived down the street...she did not want a man in her house! My uncle's main aim was 'to discipline me'...this meant a beating for any misdemeanour. Somehow, I managed to keep out of his reach but we eventually became friends when one-day he asked me if I could see Gabriel in the ackee tree. "Can you see his armour of gold?" he implored. Looking carefully into the dancing leaves of the tree, I said, "Yes, uncle." He patted me on the head and said, "If you can see Gabriel, you must be a good boy..." My Aunts, my Mother and uncle were born in New Green (named so by slave masters from Greenock, Scotland). They left school at 11 years of age. The small piece of land where they were born is called Marshalls Pen.

Aunt Hilda's tax receipt for Marshalls Pen (1985-86)

It was acquired by their ancestors from their 'owners', the Lamonds of Argyll, Scotland, at the end of slavery.

The first time I saw Marshalls Pen, the earth was broken, red and almost dead. It had been sucked dry to an inch of its long life by too many crops of colonial-grown coffee and sugar. My Mother's surname was Larmond. Her great grandfather, at the end of slavery, took his owner's surname and called himself Larmond instead of Lamond. His slave name was Henry, and when he was freed he called himself Henry Larmond. He and his male descendants described their professions as planters...a profession they regarded as important because slave masters called themselves planters. As in Scottish tradition, his Christian name, Henry, has been passed down to eldest sons, so my Mother gave me Henry as one of my names. Our names are an important part of the history of Britishness and provide a permanent link between us and the contributions our ancestors made to the British Empire. What's in a name?...a history which confers rights that cannot be changed. Henry is one of the names of my grandson. He was born in Edinburgh.

When my Mother's parents died, my Grandaunt took her sister's children (my Mother and my Aunts) to Kingston to live with her at 37 John Street in Allman Town, because the land was depleted. It could no longer support them. Allman Town is known for its poverty, but it has always been of great pride to me because Marcus Garvey (1887 - 1940), the great promoter of black potential, was a local government representative for Allman Town.

My Grandaunt used to say that our main purpose in life is to love God and to make sure that no-one suffers or dies from hunger or human cruelty. Like my Mother and my Aunts, my Grandaunt loved a good funeral. She loved the equality of death and the exclusivity of heaven. "Only the chosen-good will be admitted," she would sigh with closed eyes. My Aunts and Mother were devout Christians even though they did not disregard the powers of obeah. They saw death as the rest they worked for all their lives. My Mother came alive at family weddings and funerals. Although she was ill we travelled together to Jamaica to bury her brother. She took me to examine the coffin and prodded the lining and told the undertaker that it was not plush enough and had to be replaced. She prepared her brother for burial using a mixture of customs passed on from previous generations. I knew I would be the last generation to do this...emigration to Britain at fourteen years of age damaged the link between custom and practice in our culture.

My Aunts fed me, clothed and cared for me with a string of Victorian commands: children are to be seen and not heard...do what you are told to do...small boys don't talk back...only men wear under-pants and you are a boy...eat what you are given...don't eat from strangers, they can obeah you...don't tear your clothes... learn your three Rs, but too much learning will damage your eyes and your brain...we will feed you, teachers will teach you and the Reverend will save your soul, so saith the Lord...manners maketh the man...don't talk when you eat...honour thy Mother...sweep the yard...stain and shine the floor...haste makes waste...feed the dogs...The Lord loves obedient children...ingratitude is the worst of sins...spare the rod and spoil the child...you will go to Stoney Hill if you don't behave...keep your head up... don't bear false witness...go to bed, Big Ben and the BBC's Mr Stamp say it is 9 of the clock…say your prayers… you will get a beating if you keep saying cha (pshaw) and suck your teeth like the slaves used to do… and remember, God is not sleeping.

My Grandaunt was called *Auntie* and everyone loved and respected her. She was tall, mysterious, wore a brimmed hat on top of her grey, curly hair and she read her bible every day. Her skin was pale as moonlight and her eyes were blue-green like the sea, but my Grandaunt's sister's skin and eyes were velvet black. We all differed in colour, shape and form but the significance of such differences had no meaning until we arrived in London where the 'Keep Britain White' graffiti confirmed general antipathy to our colour and as some newspapers fanned the flames of prejudice, the 'Black Shirts' and others attacked us. Two politicians were particularly unpleasant. Powell despised us because we, a tiny powerless minority, would somehow cause 'rivers of blood'. Nabarro, a comparatively recent Citizen of the Empire, cynically resurrected the slave-derived propaganda of 'the dangers of black sexuality'. With unbridled hate he stated that white girls would destroy their families' well-being by taking home big black men to tea.

Prejudice comes in many guises: some expected, others as surprising as the racism of the late Philip Larkin, who was recorded singing with gusto and low-life malice, "Throw the Niggers out." We expect this from ignorant people but surely not from 'a poet of the people' who wrote about the rights of humanity. Racists are not born, they are made in the society which they damage. In this regard, for a white ex-football manager to call a black footballer a "lazy Nigger" and then try to excuse his dishonouring of black people by stating that he helped black footballers in the past, shows that he does not understand that it is wrong to belittle people, no matter what one has done for them.

Nigger: Where does the word come from? It came from the harrows of New World slavery. As such, white people, whether prattler or poet, should be ashamed to speak it; but black people should be proud to hear it. The word Nigger is the evidence of a great brutality that came from white slavers like Thomas Thistlewood, a friend of fellow slaver, James Wedderburn. Thistlewood was a Jamaica-based English slave master during a period of The European (Scottish) Enlightenment (1750-1786). His numerous sexual partners were black female slaves. They bore him children in between torture. He documented, in detail, his criteria for purchasing slaves: "Negroes that have big bellies, ill shaped legs, and great feet are commonly dull and sluggish and not often good; whereas those who have good calf to their leg and a small moderate size foot, are commonly nimble, active Negroes...Have also observed that many new Negroes, who are bought fat and sleek from the ship, soon fall away much in a plantation, whereas those which are in a moderate condition hold their flesh better and are commonly hardier. Those whose lips are pale, or whites of their eyes yellowish, are seldom healthy". The word Nigger came out of this evil (pages 129, 130, 131)...an evil that changed the name, Negro to Nigger. Those who use the word Nigger as a weapon of abuse are pathetic little people of low self-esteem and great ignorance.

Another prominent 'racist' during this modern period of racial torture was Sir Keith Joseph. At an interview for my first research position in 1964, he suggested that I should go back to Trinidad. I said I was from London, not Trinidad. With a blatant disregard of what I had said, he suggested that I should go there and grow bananas. Not one member of the interview panel intervened. He then asked with measured malice, "How can bananas produce new bananas when they have no seeds?" I replied slowly, "They have suckers." The mockery continued. Knowing that I had never been on a farm he asked, "What is the difference between a wheat field and a barley field?" I did not know that then! The inevitable, "I regret to inform you letter" followed. I took it with a sigh and moved on with a smile: my *system consciousness* was in the process of development.

Although I have related the above encounter with Sir Keith Joseph as many times (see Articles 11 23, 51) as I have related encounters with other people who influenced my life, in September 2015 Charles Moore (see The Spectator and see Articles 47, 48,51 52 and 53) and the CPS (Centre for Policy Studies) raked up, out of context, the comments made by Keith Joseph when he interviewed me in 1964 at Reading University. Sadly, the 'banana' comment (more a cultural insult than an illegal racist slur in 1964) was taken out of context from my interview on the Life Scientific programme, BBC Radio 4, on the 4th August 2015. The intention of this programme was to use my life experiences to help other people deal with similar life problems (51, 52, 53). However, Charles Moore published a series of statements about Sir Keith Joseph and myself in The Spectator between September and November 2015. His position, without valid evidence, was that the person at my interview who made the comments about 'farm, wheat, barley, banana and Trinidad' was not Sir Keith Joseph. On Moore's approach to evidence, he could have said, I was not present at the interview…

The CPS was formed by Sir Keith Joseph, Mrs Thatcher and Sir

Alfred Sherman the "racist" speech writer of Sir Keith in 1974. The CPS sent me a strange pre-dated latter, e-mails in response to my e-mails and a copy of one of Moore's statements attacking me which I had already seen. I also had a long phone call from Tim Knox, Director of the CPS, where-in the untenable evidence from Nottingham University was discussed and the untenable source of Moore's Nottingham evidence was revealed. Like Moore, the CPS did not investigate the relative Whitehall connections (51, 52, 53) between Reading University and Nottingham University in 1964. Although I have no idea why Sir Keith was present at my interview at Reading University, research has shown that the Chancellor of Reading University in 1964 was Lord Edward Bridges. Lord Bridges was Head of the Home Civil Service and Permanent Secretary to the Treasury. Lord Wolfenden was Vice Chancellor of the same University until 1963 and then became the Chair of the University Grants Council. The Imperial College of Agriculture in Trinidad, were *inter alia* civil servants were trained for crop management duties in the colonies, was attached to Reading University in 1964. This early Whitehall and Reading University link seems to have continued because Sir Keith Joseph, as Education Secretary, opened the Food Studies Building of the University. One of Moore's red herrings was that Sir Keith knew nothing about agriculture. This was not the case (47, 48). In addition, my application was not for a position in agriculture, it was for a positon in plant science.

My response (see Articles) to Moore's public attack in association with the CPS's private attack on me are not based on justifiable evidence. Anyone who has listened to the Life Scientific programme or read the well-known materials relating to my interview knows that it was Sir Keith's manipulative farm, wheat and barley questions that stop me getting the grant to study plant science in 1964. I dealt with the banana insult, I had no way of dealing with the manipulative farm, wheat and barley questions (11, 23, 47, 48, 51, 52 and 53).

So far, Moore and the CPS have failed to show why Sir Keith Joseph was not at my interview in 1964. The Herald (51) stated that Moore wrote that: "The Centre for Policy studies has now complained to the BBC about the programme. Sir Geoff might reflect that his account of what Joseph said would, if Sir Keith were alive, require the legal defence of justification – provable truth – to avoid losing a libel action. As a learned scientist with a regard for the truth for evidence, Sir Geoff surely feels a moral if not a legal duty to produce his." The Herald also reported that, "Moore, who revealed the complaint to the BBC, said the claims were reminiscent of a recent "tendency to let dreadful things", such as paedophilia allegations, be said about dead Tories who cannot answer back".

My response to these comments is that I know very little about "dead Tories" being subjected to "paedophilia allegations" and to "dreadful things". Much of what I know about Sir Keith Joseph I researched after I read what Charles Moore and the CPS had written and said about my BBC Radio 4 interview in August 2015. In fact, I know very little about Moore and the CPS. However, regarding Moore's request for "provable truth" from me, while presenting none himself (51), he has overlooked the fact that there is published evidence that Sir Keith Joseph was "alive" and did not "answer back" when comments relating to my interview with him (Sir Keith Joseph) were published on the front page a National newspaper…long before he died in 1994.

The newspaper report concluded that I "was turned down for a job" because "Keith Joseph" had set me up to fail by asking me about wheat and barley when I told him that I was from Jamaica and London and had never been on a farm as stated on the Life Scientific programme, 4th August, 2015. In this "provable truth" newspaper publication Sir Rhodes Boyson is also mentioned. He was headmaster of my school at Highbury, London, in the late 1960s and remained in contact with me until he died in 2012. In 1995, he gave me a signed copy of his recently published book. He was a political colleague of Sir Keith Joseph. Moore's contention that the person sitting in front of me, with a name plaque which said…Sir Keith Joseph, was not Sir Keith Joseph is now made to look ridiculous by his own "alive" criteria of so-called "provable truth" (see above quote, Herald, 51) because long before Sir Keith Joseph died in 1994 a National newspaper stated on its front page that Keith Joseph was at my interview in 1964. Today, Sir Keith Joseph's manipulation (54) of my interview would not only be regarded as racist, it could be regarded as an abuse that was worse than racism.

I will reveal the reference to this published evidence to Charles Moore and the CPS when they, for reasons of "proven truth" and of "moral if not legal duty" publish their evidence from Nottingham University (47, 48, 51) which Moore tried to use to show that Sir Keith was not the person at my interview. There will be great concern about their moral values if this evidence is not published in full by them.

How did I deal with this unpresented prejudicial attack on me? I dealt with it sensibly using system consciousness, some education, the memories of those who helped me and with a smile and hope…

Hope that witnessed Oliver Letwin's (a Senior Minister of the

Government) unreserved apology in December 2015, for his "badly worded and wrong" directives, in which he stated unfairly in 1985, that government funding should not be given to some Caribbean people who, like me, have been historically British for over 300 years. This prejudgement has been described as "ignorant and deeply racist views". This unfair directive from Letwin did not surprise me because I am aware that such prejudices are the invisible and visible social poisons that wreck people's lives. In terms of my encounter with Keith Joseph in 1964, it is worth mentioning that Letwin's early political career was fostered by Sir Keith Joseph in the early 1980s. Oliver Letwin became an 'adviser' to Sir Keith. Later as an MP he gave the CPS's 2002 Sir Keith Joseph's memorial lecture…in it he said, "…each individual has a personal history, of which each is as much the author as the subject". As a deduction from this it must then be very wrong for anyone to manipulate negatively and prejudicially the 'personal histories' of those who are entitled to some help to progress.

Gradually, it became clear to me that social justice cannot be achieved without an understanding of how the system works. Also, it was evident that the most dangerous people in society are those who are in a position to make a difference but prevent others from achieving. Why is achievement important? It produces tolerance. For example, I once stopped my car at a pedestrian crossing to allow an adult white male to cross. He crossed slowly, then turned back. He stood in front of my car and made the symbol of a 'rifle' with his arms and aimed it at me, pulling his forefinger forward and backwards as if firing his 'rifle'. I sat still. After he had moved, I drove away slowly avoiding him; thankfully my general achievement in education helps me to deal with hate like that.

It has been distressing to realise that ignorance of the concept of Britishness can cause apparently fair-minded people to behave and vote in a racist manner. Denial of the basic concept of Britishness, which embodies differences in race and culture and reflects historical links rather than skin colour, will destroy the meaning of Britishness. Such dangerous disregard for democracy and fairness has stifled the development of peace and trust in the community. At that time we, who were proud of our British heritage, were paid less and charged more to live and the racists, with their contrary logic, labelled us: job-takers, slum-makers, house owners, aggressive ganja scroungers with loud music, prone to insanity, susceptible to arrest, religious and educationally sub-normal. Black parents' enthusiasm for education was seriously damaged by white teachers, who dismissed their hopes for their children as 'unrealistic expectations'.

Attempts to meet the educational needs of black children were viewed in some quarters as 'unfair benefits to foreigners', in social situations where low expectations were the norm. Sadly, these unjust and jealous reactions are still at the centre of present day racist response to the legitimate rights of ethnic people. Irrespective of colour, class or creed, children tend to perform below their educational potential if negative attitudes pervade their schools and where they live.

My expectations were modest on the day I arrived at the Liverpool Docks on the Cunard line ship, *Ascania*, in 1955. I was fourteen years old and my passport said that I was a citizen of the British Empire. My trip started at the Palisadoes airport in Jamaica. I was too young to leave Jamaica alone by ship but I was permitted to fly to New York and board the *Ascania* from there. I had not been to the airport before and had only ever seen a plane flying overhead. On the night of my departure my Grandaunt called me to her rocking chair. The dogs were asleep and the house was quiet. She put down her newspaper and said a prayer and anointed my head with oil. She then told me to remove my shirt. She picked up her newspaper, *The Daily Gleaner,* and wrapped it round my chest and tied it in place with sisal string. I then replaced my shirt, took up my small suitcase and jumped on the back of Mr. Green's truck. My Aunts sat on the veranda and said nothing. I cannot remember if they waved but I knew they would miss me and that I would miss them. Our response to this parting was not displayed in hugs and kisses, we did not show our feelings in public or private.

At the Palisadoes airport I jumped down from the back of the truck and eventually I was on the plane. It was very large and had four propeller-driven engines. Many of the people spoke a language I did not understand. I had not heard a foreign language before. The newspaper under my shirt and the heat of the plane caused me to sweat and by the time we arrived in Florida I was soaking wet. They told us to get off the plane. I had not seen so many lights before. They lined us up in the half-light and began asking questions: Are you a communist? Have you ever been to a communist gathering? Do you know any communists? The man in front of me said no, so I said no. We re-boarded the plane. In New York it was very cold. Steam came out of the streets. There were about twenty four Jamaicans on the plane. They confined us to a cage-like enclosure.

One of my Mother's sisters who lived in New York threw me

her husband's overcoat over the fence. I was shaking and the wet newspaper round my chest began to get very cold. I put on the overcoat and could hardly walk because it was too long. They herded us, stumbling, onto a bus and drove us towards the ship. I had never seen so many cars before. When we arrived at the Hudson River Docks, a guard with a machine gun, whose job it was to prevent us from escaping into America, opened the back door of the bus and told us to get out and walk through Immigration. I eventually found my bed on the boat. There were six of us to a room on the bottom deck of the ship. I went to the toilet and removed the wet newspaper from my chest; my Grandaunt would certainly not know what I had done!

The *Ascania* sailed down the Hudson river past the Statue of Liberty and out to sea. The sea was rough. We were sick many times and could not eat the food, which was mainly pasta. One Jamaican man continually asked me, "What is this kind of food?" I said that I did not know. We sailed and docked at our first port…some of us thought we had arrived in Liverpool but later learned that this port was Nova Scotia. I got off the ship and walked on snow for the first time. The snow was so deep that they had to cut it away to show the windows and doors of the shops. The whole place looked like a giant Christmas card. I made and threw a snowball as I had seen people do in a film. I returned to the ship and we sailed for Liverpool. The sea boiled with anger and the ship tilted from side to side and some of us on the lowest deck of the ship nearly died from vomiting.

As we sailed towards Liverpool, I began to explore the upper decks of the ship. Only white people occupied the upper decks. When they were not gambling they were eating or dancing. One day a lady called me into a large room, she was playing cards with other ladies. Another lady put me on her knee and asked me if I was hungry. I said yes. She wrapped up a tray full of sandwiches and a tray full of pieces of fruit cake and gave them to me. I took these down to my Jamaican friends and we ate the cake and sandwiches quickly. I made my trip to the upper deck almost daily. Each time I brought back a bounty of cake and sandwiches. About ten days after leaving New York the ship reached Cork. It did not dock, it anchored out at sea. Many Irish people sailed out in small boats to meet the ship and they tried to sell us beads and trinkets! It became dark and we sailed for Liverpool with great apprehension and arrived there on the 10th March 1955...coincidentally, the 10th March is the same day, that I was given the honour, fifty years later, to return to Kingston, Jamaica, to address the Jamaica Chamber of Commerce.

After we left the docks at Liverpool, I went through Immigration with my small twenty six shillings suitcase. My grey-blue overcoat dragged on the ground as I walked. At Immigration I was asked if I had any guns or drugs. I said no. As we boarded the train I could still see the steep wall of the ship. I found a seat on the ship-train and stared out of the window as it sliced its way quickly through the flowing countryside. Soon we arrived at a large station in London. It was crowded and noisy and I stood in the half-light and looked around until a lady came and grabbed my arm with the words, "Godfrey, come with me, I am your Mother…" I did not recognise her because she left Jamaica when I was eight years old and now I was fourteen years and eleven months old.

We boarded a red bus and got off at Pentonville Prison, Caledonian Road in North London. The falling snow soaked into my flimsy shoes before we reached the front door where my Mother lived. It was very dark and my Mother could not find the hole in the door to insert the key. The landlord said hello and my Mother took me up three flights of stairs to her attic room. She turned on the light and lit the paraffin heater. Her bed was against one wall and my bed was against the opposite wall. She went out to the stair landing where the cooker was, shooed a rat that was curled up asleep on the cooker and then cooked corn beef and rice, which I ate before I brushed my teeth and went to sleep. My Mother read her Bible, said her prayers and then went to bed. I had not said my prayers from the day I left Jamaica. I said goodnight but did not know what to call her…this is just one small way in which the need to make a living disrupts the lives of poor people.

The next morning, the clock's alarm went at 6.00 a.m. My Mother switched on the light and shouted at me to get up. She turned on the radio to confirm the time and prepared herself for work. After washing, I got dressed, ate two slices of bread, drank a mug of real (green) tea and followed my Mother down the stairs in silence. Most of the other tenants in the house had already gone to work. My Mother opened the front door…a white man barred our way. He was dressed in a pinstripe suit and carried a brown briefcase. It was about 6.45 a.m. "Is the name of this boy, Godfrey Palmer ?" asked the man. "Yes," replied my Mother. "Where are you going ?" asked the man. "To work," said my Mother. "You can go to work, but the boy cannot," he warned. "Why not?" asked my Mother. "Because he is not fifteen years of age, and in this country all children have to go to school until they are at least fifteen…is that clear?"

My Mother realised that her plans to take me to work had failed and she began to beg the man to be lenient. She implored, "I, Sir, have been in this country since 1948. I have worked nights sorting mailbags for less than three pounds ten shillings a week. Now I only have two pounds ten shillings a week to live on and, I have this boy in London to feed and another younger boy in Jamaica to feed and I do not have a man to help me. My son's fare to London cost me £86 and this took me from 1948 to 1955 to save…my son has to work to help me." "He can get a paper round…or a Saturday job, but he must go to school…I don't make the rules," he concluded, firmly.

He gave my Mother a piece of paper on which the names of various schools were written. That same day my Mother took me to Barnsbury Comprehensive School and they gave me a test and the results indicated that I was 'educationally sub-normal'. I was sent to Shelburne Road Secondary Modern and they accepted me.

Mr. Bullen was the Headmaster of Shelburne Road School. He took me on the grounds that I would stay longer than the month required to take me to my fifteenth birthday in April, because he did not want me to 'ruin the Register'! It was agreed that I stayed until June 1955. At Shelburne, some parents abused some teachers and some teachers smirked at the poor abilities of the pupils and some pupils fought each other at break-time. It was the time of the Teddy boy gangs and I used my experience of the streets in Jamaica to avoid trouble. There was an ease about education at Shelburne.

In one 'maths' lesson we had to cut out pictures of furniture, give them prices then add up the total cost. The music teacher was wolf-whistled when she came into the room and the old history teacher started many lessons by glaring at the teddy boys. He would then repeat, "At the war front, it was the bullies that were afraid to fight." At that time 'racism' was directed mainly at the Jews. The main derogatory comment in the playground was, 'You dirty Jewboy'. However, in a short while this seemed to change to 'Coon' and 'You bloody Nigger'.

At Shelburne I excelled at scripture and cricket but it was cricket that played the most significant part in changing my life. Two months after joining Shelburne I was playing cricket in the playground. The games-master stopped me and said that I should meet him after school on Wednesday. On Wednesday he gave me a pair of white gym shoes and he took me, by train, to a place called Gants Hill. It was a large park and there were many boys there accompanied by their parents carrying large cricket bags. I did not understand the purpose of this event but I was asked to bowl and bat which I did. The games-master and I left and returned home. Two weeks later, I was called by the games-master, who told me calmly, "You have been selected to play for London...you are now a member of the London Schoolboys Cricket Team (see page 138)..."

The games master gave me a white shirt and white flannels he had collected, and another teacher gave me a pair of white canvas boots. The fixtures of the team included: Eton, Harrow, Winchester and Middlesex Colts. The significance of these names escaped me at the time. I merely turned up, went on long coach rides, played cricket and returned home to Bride Street which was near Pentonville Prison. The vastness of the playing fields at Eton was exciting and I have not forgotten the boy who looked after me at Harrow. I was allocated to him when I got off the coach. He said, "Hello," and asked if I would like to see his dorm…I said, "Yes," but did not quite know what he meant. As we walked across the grass I thought that this must be a school for poor boys because he had a straw hat…to me this view was confirmed fully when he showed me where he slept ! There were many iron bunk beds in the room, the floor was wooden and not even covered with linoleum. It was fairly cold…and not a paraffin heater in sight. He asked me, "And what does your daddy do ?" I replied cheerfully, "Well he is in New York and I have been told he runs numbers…a sort of a gambling racket." "Ah," he said, in great astonishment, "My Daddy does the same…he's in the City." We had a good game at Harrow and we won.

Like the Church, the game of cricket filled me with awe and worry. I did not have a scrapbook of The Apostles but I had a large scrapbook of great cricketers and tried to copy the different styles in which they played the game. I had only ever watched two days of test match cricket during my childhood in Jamaica. Both times I was helped to climb over the high wall of the Sabina Park cricket ground. I was one of a large group of boys who were trying to get over the wall because we had no money.

The only price I paid to watch these matches was a twisted ankle because the jump down, into the grounds, was about ten feet. I saw the West Indies play England. Of the cricketers I saw in Jamaica, I will never forget the grace of Frank Worrell and Len

Hutton; the craft of Denis Compton; the power of Everton Weeks and the controlled aggression of Clyde Walcott. Nor will I forget the safe hands of Godfrey Evans, the smooth running and delivery of Hines Johnson; the erratic speed of Freddie Trueman; the accuracy of Alec Bedster and Lance Gibbs, and the magical spin bowling of Sonny Ramadhin. I also had the special privilege to see the last test match of the great George Headly. He had passed his best and made only one run.

Cricket can be elating but there is the dark side of the game. All those who have played cricket are aware of its terrors…the nervous knee-shaking walk to the wicket, the intimidation of the fielders, the being out for nought, the slow long walk back to the silence of team members that one has let down, the dropped catch and the thrashing received without taking a wicket. Then there was the minister of the Church that acted as umpire. He sent me off the field for 'technical dissent'. When I complained that I was never sent off in Jamaica for dissent…he smiled and said, "You do here!" All these hazards of the game conspired to convince me that hereafter I should only play this very British game, that changed my life for the better, for pleasure.

In July or August 1955, the Islington Gazette published an article which said that Shelburne had produced a valuable schoolboy cricketer that was playing for London. Mr. King, the headmaster of the local grammar school must have seen the article and asked Mr. Bullen, the headmaster of Shelburne, to transfer me to Highbury County School. My Mother was again disappointed that the grocery boy's job she had arranged for me would fall through but accepted the £5 per term which she received to help pay for my school uniform which I was required to wear at Highbury.

Before I went to Highbury, I got a temporary job, to supplement my paper round money, at Fasbender and Evans, a leather handbag firm, in the East End of London. I lined sections of handbags with satin. Each day the foreman would pick five of us from the work floor and send us to the toilet for 'rest periods'. When I asked him why we had to do this, he replied firmly, "To save jobs, Sunshine…to save jobs." I left the job to go to Highbury School at the beginning to the Autumn term of 1955.

When I entered Highbury, I was the only black pupil. When I left in 1958 there were two black pupils, a boy called Michael Phillips and me. He was from Guyana and told us that he knew Latin. The only other pupils from the Empire at the school were Theofanides and Papapetrou - they were Greek-Cypriots. Osman was a Turkish-Cypriot and Cardozo was from Burma. Phillips did not play cricket or football. Theo and Papa played football. We were all of the British Empire and we got on well but the Cypriots argued bitterly over Cyprus.

Mr King, the headmaster, knew how we were affected by local hardships and the politics of the British Empire. This may have influenced him in permitting us to put on a dance in the school. We made a large profit and bought the school a small silver cup out of part of the profit! We called it the Commonwealth Cup. I have been told that Highbury now has mainly ethnic pupils and a cup called the Commonwealth Cup is given for team work.

Mr. King was a kindly man and devoted himself to the education of deprived children. He allowed me to run two paper rounds from which I earned £1 per week. I gave my Mother ten shillings, sent three shillings to my Grandaunt in Jamaica and kept seven shillings for my lunch and spending money. Instead of throwing out 'slow learners and troublemakers', he assembled them in a special class called The Removes. I was in The Removes and so were most of my friends, except a boy called Bob Green who has remained a very close friend. Bob introduced me to beer and I introduced him to the music of Shirley and Lee and other Blues singers. Nearly all the members of the school's cricket and football teams came from The Removes. Our maths teacher, Mr Lewis, disliked us and often humiliated us by asking us to solve problems we could not solve. One day he stopped me in the playground and said, "Where are you from, boy?" "Jamaica, sir." " Must be hot there in Africa this time of year, what, what!" "Yes, sir…" Unlike Mr Lewis, Corporal (Mr) Gage, the games master, was more charitable. He called all of us 'dirty scumbags' because our gym shoes were dirty! When I told him that my Mother did not want me to swim because of an ear ache, he retorted, "Do I tell your Mother how to bake a cake!" I never did learn to swim.

My academic performance at Highbury was patchy. I was not familiar with the concepts of science subjects such as chemistry, physics and mathematics and struggled to cope but I did reasonably well at scripture, history, geography and biology. Achievement in science required experience which I did not have but I liked English Literature mainly because one of our teachers, Mr. Ward, made us muddle through Steinbeck, Hemingway and Faulkner in the class, whether we liked it or not. It took me some time to understand what he was trying to do but having had to read the Bible all my life, the stories of these writers probably made more sense to me than they did to some of the other boys. However, the main purpose of my 'transfer' to Highbury was to play cricket and football and this I did frequently and relatively well!

My school days at Highbury ended in 1958. I had passed a few 'O' level and two 'A' level examinations. Of the many events that happened at Highbury, I will remember that my friend Bob and I were among London children sent to the country for a few days to broaden their outlook of Britain. Roaming around the streets of a town called Oswestry, Bob and I went into a pet shop and ordered two birds…he wanted an archaeopteryx and I wanted a pterodactyl. The owner smiled at us quizzically and after searching through a book said, "We have had a run on these…very popular these foreign birds…but we can get them in if you wish." "No sir," we said, "we are leaving the country soon." The biology teacher then enquired at the counter what we were up to. He was not amused and threatened to cane us to within an inch of our lives. I left school before my luck ran out! Bob went to work for the Bank of West Africa somewhere in London but did not stay long. He is now Chairman of his own company in the United States. I did not have a job so I went to the Islington Public Library every day, except Sundays, to read the papers and keep warm. Incidentally, in 2014, just as Her Majesty the Queen kindly conferred the honour of Knighthood on me at Holyrood Palace in Edinburgh, Bob, who had flown in from Philadelphia for the ceremony, leant forward in his seat and said, "Yes." One word for all the ups and downs of a lifetime.

I have been told many times, "You must have worked hard to achieve what you have achieved." Hard work, without support from others is not enough to make significant gains in life, especially in education. I have had the help of many 'Good Samaritans' in my life. One was Professor Garth Chapman. He gave me my first job in 1958. I was a junior technical assistant at Queen Elizabeth College. I did odd jobs in the department. He encouraged me to discuss the difficulties, which were causing my poor attendance at work. The Prof. understood how people like myself had to live so he refused to confirm my dismissal. When he realised that, at eighteen, I was defending my Mother in court from being evicted from our home, he encouraged me to study the function of the court and the meaning of the rent act. We won the case. The landlord had to stop the continual noise, re-connect our water supply and desist from starting fights. Indeed, the bucket I used to collect our daily drinking and washing water from across the road now grows plants. Our rent was half my Mother's wage which was five pounds per week. She worked as a dress finisher for Mr. Kafka in the East End of London, and received a box of Woolworths' chocolate at Christmas, if she did not miss a day's work during the year.

After we won the court case, the Prof. said that I should complete my university entrance examinations and try to enter university by 1961. I did not want to go to university to fail. I did not know how I would relate with people who did not have my background. Passing the racists at Notting Hill Gate each day on my way to and from work, was less of a problem. During this period, I did not know any West Indian students. They wore scarves and told white people that they were different from us immigrants. But after the riots in Notting Hill Gate (1958) they became immigrants because white racists treated us all the same…black was black! When I failed to secure a place in any university in Britain Professor Chapman argued my case and consequently I got a place at Leicester University in 1961. Seeds will not find furrows and grow in impossible soil…likewise, my efforts alone were not enough even though I had met the entrance requirements of various universities and held a County Major Grant Award from the London County Council. Before I left my job for Leicester, the Prof., with the anger of the just, advised me thus, "In future, never send a photograph with any application form. This contrivance should not be necessary in a civilised society but it may induce prejudiced people to read at least part of your application form before they reject you!" Despite the concept that the rights of the minority must not conflict with the expectations of the majority, a true democracy exists to defend the rights of both the majority and the minority. Professor Chapman was a great egalitarian. Sadly he died in 2003 not knowing that in 2016 when I gave my acceptance speech for the Honorary Doctor of Science degree that was offered to me by Leicester University, I did refer to his role in getting me a place at the University in 1961 and likened his kindness to the older leaves, of the plants in my undergraduate project experiment, which passed their nutrients to younger leaves before they wilted and died in drought conditions…nature's lesson in the meaning of goodness.

I returned to London after gaining my first degree at Leicester University in Botany in 1964. I did not know what my degree qualified me to do. One of my friends from the streets reasoned that Botany was like gardening and suggested that I asked at Finsbury Park what kind of work was available. I decided to work with my Uncle Se, the husband of Aunt Kate. Uncle Se had a house in Marlborough Road and most of the family lived in the house...my Mother and I did not. He loved Scotch whisky and his work. However, he was not pleased that in Jamaica he was called a carpenter but in London he was called a joiner! We did many different kinds of work: cleaning sewers, plastering, wood and cement work and decorating. I helped but had no expertise at all. It is difficult to recount all the jobs we completed but I remember filling gaping holes in dusty wattle walls with newspapers and plastering them into the wall. I became more and more nervous regarding the quality of our work and finally 'resigned' when a night club owner threatened to kill us because his heavy Hessian (Japanese) wall paper fell off the wall after two days... Uncle Se's view was that we were lucky, the owner would have killed us had he paid us! After Uncle Se's house was damaged mysteriously by bottles, and the police failed to respond to our call, I decided that my career as a decorator was over and my search for a real job began at the Seven Sisters Road Labour Exchange in London.

At the partition grid of the Labour Exchange, I was questioned by a man. He exuded that kind of indifference that numbs the mind. He looked at me and smirked, "Any skills, any qualifications?" I said that I had a degree. He rocked on his chair and laughed. Turning to his colleague he sniggered, "Hi here, Paddy, this one reckons he has a temperature!" He gave me a slip of paper...one job was for a park attendant in Finsbury Park, the other job was for a potato peeler at Beales restaurant in Holloway Road, London.

At Beales, the old lady who peeled the potatoes told me that this job would get me far. She had done it for thirty years and because I looked a bright boy there were no good reasons why I could not do it for a similar period. I enjoyed my job at Beales. Among the many things I learnt, I remember two vividly: one of the cooks admonished me because I was about to throw away a bowl of fruit salad that had been returned by a customer. He took the bowl containing the limp-looking fruit salad and added a bright red cherry to the centre of the fruit salad in the bowl and sent it back down to the restaurant…the same customer ate the fruit salad and did not complain. The cook then smiled at me and said, "Most people judge on appearance, mate… they usually see what they want to see, not what is there…get my drift!" The other lesson I learnt was that when the same cook asked for 'new potatoes' he meant that I should hunt through the damp mound of 'old potatoes' to find 'small old potatoes'! I applied for many jobs during my time at Beales (see Articles 47, 48 and BBC, Life Scientific, 2015) and was finally accepted at the Heriot-Watt College (now a University) and Edinburgh University in 1964 by Professor Anna MacLeod, to study for a joint PhD in grain science (see Page 127) and technology, at the beginning of 1965.

I met many West Indian students in Edinburgh. They were high achievers who came directly to universities in Britain and usually returned to the West Indies after completing their studies. The late Bernie Grant, who became a Member of Parliament for the Labour Party, did not return to Guyana. He went from Edinburgh to London and established himself as a prominent politician in the area of race relations. The last time Bernie came to Edinburgh was to discuss the entry of his son into university. Before he left for London we had a drink in a pub in Duddingston. Sadly, the higher fees paid by overseas students have almost stopped this tradition in Higher education where the professionals and leaders of many countries of the old British Empire were educated in Britain. These high fees have not only reduced the influence which British education had in the world, they have also diminished the rich cultural mix that is an important element of any university. I completed successfully my Post-graduate and Post-doctoral studies in Edinburgh and started my research career as a grain scientist at a research institute in Surrey, England, in 1968.

For unknown reasons providence has enabled me to avoid or manage the malice and nonsense of racists. In this regard, a minor incident comes to mind. In 1971, I was invited to an International Conference in Portugal to present a piece of my research work. The work described an invention in grain processing which was in use in the industry. I returned to Heathrow (London) with a group of British colleagues. My colleagues passed easily through Immigration. I was told to wait. The young officer was not convinced that I was with the group. After a difficult debate with the young man, my boss, Dr A H Cook FRS approached us and said, "Do what you must, Palmer but remember that logic is wasted on the illogical." The officer retreated and stamped my passport. On the coach I opened my passport and noticed that he had stamped... 'Visitor for 3 months'. Such incidents can occur at any time and black people have had to learn to live with unpredictable abuse. However, such incidents serve the useful purpose of illustrating the general state of thinking of sections of the community. There is little doubt that ignorance is a major factor in racism and that education and common respect in the community can limit the damaging effects of this disease.

The negative perception of the 'Black Outsider' is still prevalent in our society. For example, recently, I was in the reception area of a large legal institution to attend a meeting. I asked the receptionist to inform the person that I had come to see that I had arrived. After some considerable time my colleague came to the reception area to collect me. He then told me that when he asked the receptionist if Professor Palmer had arrived, he was told, "No, Professor Palmer has not yet arrived…but there is some black guy waiting to see you!" Another irritating but equally silly encounter occurred recently on a train to London where I was asked to give a lecture on education and race. A man grabbed my arm complaining about seat reservations. Before I could respond his friend whispered in his ear, "John, John, he is not the bloody porter!"

To recount all such encounters would be a waste of time. However, each encounter helps to illustrate the complexity of the racial attitudes that infect our society. For example, some time ago, on my return from promoting my institution abroad I was informed that my white colleagues had held a meeting against me. When I asked one of them why he had been involved in this he replied, "What could I do, I was up for promotion?" What disappointed me most was that not one of these 'educated' people said, "This is wrong, I want no part in it." In another similar incident the only comment from a white colleague was, "How the hell do you put up with things like that?" My response was, "With the best weapon allowed… *education!*"

That people like myself should require the help of 'Good Samaritans' to achieve what they could have achieved on their own is a sad indication of the damage that small, mean-minded people do to our institutions. Institutions are not racist, people are. Such people neither respect the law nor the concept of Britishness. They elected racist politicians in the 1960s and despite the growth in the small voice of anti-racism over the years; in 2009 these people continue to elect racist politicians such as those in the BNP (British National Party) to represent them on British Councils and in the Parliament of Europe. To them race laws are political palliatives that can be ignored and Britishness only applies to white people. To make lasting progress, the 'good people' of the system should let racists, of any kind, know that the evil they practice will not be tolerated.

Of the numerous concerns we had as British Subjects, the greatest ones were that many 'good people' said that racist politicians such as Powell and Nabarro were right, and that our *Mother Country and Church were silent*. In response to these disappointments we formed prayer meetings and we danced, when we could, to the music of our Sound Systems. Our jobs paid our way, but we were sustained by our prayers, music and a historical sense of belonging... all products of our African-British (Jamaican) heritage. We called each other *Brother-man* and *Sister Chile*, to re-assure each other because we knew that where there is no sense of belonging damaged lives are found. To sideline community crimes as 'black-on-black' or 'Afro-Caribbean' crimes is unwise, because such narrow views divide the community further along insoluble racial lines. *Punish the guilty, not the people*. From any quarter, punish those who prey on others because it is easy. Racial differences or difficulties are not excuses for criminality.

Stereotyping increases prejudice. For example, the term 'Afro-Caribbean' is not equivalent to 'Afro-American'.

In the media, it depicts negative skin colour rather than nationality and should be removed from serious useage. We must not approve inappropriate labels that undermine our nationalities and black identity (see articles 13,14, 15 and Epilogue). Thankfully, the tendency for human beings to use skin colour to erect social barriers is often matched by the capacities of human beings to transcend such prejudice. A few years ago I arrived at Harwich to board a ferryboat to Holland to give a lecture on barley and malt. As I left the crowded train, I realised that I had left my passport in Edinburgh. The port official told me that I would not be allowed to travel. Just as I was about to leave, a chanting came from the crowd behind me: "Let him on, let him on, let him on." I turned and noticed that the chanting came from a host of young men wearing green and white scarves...they were Celtic Football Supporters. The police and the port officials formed a circle to discuss the matter. To my astonishment I was given a temporary travel document. It was not until the crowd of young men had hoisted me onto the boat and into the bar that I realised the reason for their protest. They had mistaken me for a Celtic Football Supporter...I was wearing a green velvet jacket! Somehow, this football encounter has contributed to my belief that humanity has the compassion to transcend the damaging social barriers that wicked people have constructed from skin colour. Although this gesture of support may merely reflect the importance of common identity in group behaviour, improvements in human relationships depend on the goodness that motivates people to defend the rights of others. It has often worried me why, so few people, took so long, before they agreed that New World slavery was wrong...

I was about ten years old when Reverend died and I was in the 'big-children' part of the Church School. Singing and scripture were the main subjects. Punishment for misbehaving during these lessons was severe. The beating strap was made of leather and had five fingers and, like our spoons and trains, was *Made in Britain*. Curiously we were proud of this branding and believed it to be the best. Reverend Nichol told us many stories from the Bible. He also told us that there was slavery in Jamaica and at one time Jamaica had many thousands of slaves… many thousands more than were present in America. I used to ask him, "What was slavery?" He always gave the same answer, "Slavery was a long and cruel silence and a bad mistake…my mistake." "How did that mistake happen?" I would ask, and he always gave the same answer, "No one knows, but mistakes happen and they may be God's way of showing people that cruelty is not only wrong, it produces terrible consequences."

This puzzled me and I started to dream about New World slavery and how the Reverend and I fitted into this human tragedy…a tragedy that has been underestimated with regard to its cruelty and denied with regard to its terrible consequences, then and now. A tragedy that has produced lynching, social isolation, poverty and abuse. However, to black people, the only thing worse than this tragedy is its denial.

Today I am very much older and childhood dreams have turned into sad and happy experiences. Thankfully, we can be changed by education. As a boy in London, I was asked the time by a white neighbour who believed that black people were backward. "What's the time, little African?" he asked mockingly, pointing to the sun. I looked towards the sun and said, "Ten minutes past three." Covertly, he looked at his watch and confirmed that my time was correct! Many weeks later we passed each other in the street. We both nodded and he muttered the apology, "Good on you, son!"

About forty five years later, as an adult in Edinburgh, two little boys followed me around a paper shop for a while pointing at me, the younger boy said, "Look, there is a nigger." The older boy slapped him on the head and said, "It is rude to point..." Surely, if white children can be taught not to point at adults, they can be taught not to call them niggers - racism is learnt not inherited.

Ignorance and prejudice produce nasty people that mock and abuse other people because of differences in colour and culture. Without doubt, we have all been damaged by the holocaust of New World slavery, for we all know the negative images of black people that have come from that evil event. Without question, we are bound together forever in this historical marriage which cannot be dissolved and therefore must succeed. These may seem hard truths to swallow, but then, historical truths only offend the unjust, who peddle hate, unfairness and division in the community.

In *The Enlightenment Abolished narrative* (page 58) there are no tables or figures to show profit from slavery or the high price of slaves. There are no reproductions of *Run Away* notices depicting shackled humans either on ancient ships or in strange fields reaping sugar cane, coffee, corn, cotton, tobacco or spices, for 'masters' with whips and guns. We have seen these terrible images many times and it is worrying that many people are becoming inured to them and that some people have used them, without respect, to even 'adorn' commercial wallpaper. However, despite the historical importance of these images one question must be...do they convey the *tragic consequences* of slavery? Despite the historical importance of these images they essentially incite emotion. However, what is needed is an insight into life and death during our slavery and how they affect us all today.

The legacies of our slavery are various and difficult to define. Unlike other human tragedies its wickedness is made worse by the ignorance that denies a shared history. It is unfortunate that New World slavery has contributed to what racists regard as, 'earned cultural rights' to castigate others debilitated and put in doubt by the same historical circumstances. However, no living person has personally 'earned' culture and citizenship. These are bestowed by accidents of history, birth or by the law. Therefore, it is misguided for anyone to boast about the legacy of a terrible crime that still offends.

Recently, it has been proposed that multiculturalism is a limitation to the development of Britishness and should be discontinued as a concept. This is incorrect. Multiculturalism teaches social co-existence: Britishness embodies political belonging. Both concepts complement each other to produce citizens with equal rights and responsibilities. The greatest limitation to the development of citizenship is not muticulturalism, it is the word race. It is divisive in every context in which it is used and should be abolished. For example the words *race relations* should be replaced by the words *human relations*. Citizenship is more important than which team one cheers for in sport. Citizenship is a sense of belonging that comes from the feeling that rights are equal and that the system is fair and accessible. Without a sense of belonging even good people can turn into monsters. Incidentally, many Scottish and Welsh people do not cheer for England in sport but are not disloyal to the country... If multiculturalism is to continue to have a positive role in society, the contributions made by all the people of the British Empire to Britishness should be taught and admired. Without admiration there can be no resolution to racial prejudice.

Despite political footwork to appease culture-phobics, the concept of *Diversity* is *Multiculturalism* by another name. If words such as diversity and ethnic (minority) are used mainly with regard to non-white people, they will take on the connotation of 'Outsiders' and lose their purpose and universality of meaning. The sameness of humanity is greater than its differences. That I was asked if I would change the title of a lecture on 'Ethnic Foods' to 'Foods from Afar' indicates how people avoid facing important issues by spurious changing of words.

Irrespective of skin colour: those with their copied arrogance and smugness should become tolerant and fair: those with their doubts and fears should not react by damaging themselves or, through their actions, confirm negative stereotypes that diminish other people. In many ways, what we are reflects the pride of past victories and the humiliations of past defeats. This should not be overlooked if we are to understand each other. For some to dismiss the concerns of others as, 'chip on the shoulder' or 'thin skin', is disgraceful.

One dangerous consequence that has come from the word race is that some people, have tried, unsuccessfully, to turn social differences into genetic differences. This is the 'proof' racists need to justify the nonsense that skin colour and the shape and form of human beings indicate differences in intelligence and worth. The racist concepts of intelligence that have been drawn from the book, *The Bell Curve* or from the work and views of Eysenck, Jensen and Watson are scientifically worthless because they were derived from surveys which had no controls. In addition, those 'researchers' that have been involved in this kind of puerile racial propaganda, have never understood the relevance of scientific control. Without proper controls, research results are meaningless. In this regard, a proper control group, to any black group descended from slaves, should be whites that have been subjected to black enslavement for over 400 years. Since this concept is unthinkable, research that tries to show that social differences between black and white people are of genetic origins should be disregarded because historical and demographic differences render such comparisons unscientific. It is nonsense to compare the academic performance of under-privileged children with those of privileged children of any ethnic group. Such kinds of dangerous propaganda masquerading as science would not be tolerated in any other area of scientific research.

The neglect and indifference shown by many learned institutions to education and race, as a serious subject of study, has contributed to the damaging perception that 'race relations' is criminal activity associated with the police and black people. In this regard, the war against racism should not only be waged against those in the police who are racists, it should also be waged, with equal rage, against others engaged in the foul practise of racism.

New World slavery was never peaceful and there were many moments of human defiance. Two come to mind. One such moment was in 1760 when a Jamaican slave, who was being *slow-burned* for 'impudence' threw a burning log from the fire that consumed him, at his 'owner' and executioner. The other was in 1782 when Admiral Rodney, with 36 British ships against 34 superior French and Spanish ships, won the Battle of the Glorious 12th of April in the Caribbean, to keep Jamaica and other Caribbean islands, British. Even as slaves we fought for Britain against the French. Then we were more important than kith and kin in the American colonies but now, all we want are our human rights so that we can compete equally. Robert Burns, who was fond of Jamaica and knew its value to the British Empire, was not a man to waste words on what was not relevant to the human condition. He toasted the victory of Rodney thus: "Here's to the Memory of those on the Twelfth we lost! We lost, did I say? No, by Heaven that we found! For their fame it shall live while the world goes round…" This victory secured Britain's dominance and wealth in the Caribbean and paved the way for Nelson's victory at Trafalgar, 23 years later. In my dream we are all in the fire and on Rodney's ships and share the same defiance of the enemy. It should be noted that the defiance of the unknown Jamaican slave that was murdered by burning was of the same heroic kind as that of Leonidas of Ancient Greece.

There are some who believe that Britishness is an unpalatable legacy of the past and should be forgotten and replaced. But how can we replace history? Among other things, history reminds us of the contributions and rights of the people that make up the communities of the world. Like many of the people of Jamaica, my Mother was proud of her country's contribution and connection to Britishness. This Britishness belongs equally to those who were slaves and those who were masters. She was proud and pleased that I would go to Buckingham Palace to receive an OBE from the Queen for my contribution to grain science. She told everyone in the hospital. Sadly, after 56 years in Britain she died on the 9th of December, 2003, the day before I received the award. Before she died she reminded me that the award was a symbol not bad money. To reject such a collective award one would need the permission of all those who have contributed to the award. My Mother also added that anyone who is a product of Britishness and advocates abolition of this award does not understand that history affects us all differently. To change the name of the award would be humbug because if one "gives back" *Empire* awards one should also "give back" *Empire* benefits. She was also suspicious of the motives of those who turn down an award in public when it could have been refused in private. Values are not made or changed by awards.

After I accepted the OBE award at the Palace, London, a band played melodic music in the large red-carpeted room. Amid the splendour, I could see ancestors slaving in ripe cane and coffee fields hoping that their hopes would be fulfilled. The award is their achievement, not mine. After the award ceremony I was congratulated by a stranger from Edinburgh, who asked, "Are you a member of the society?" Not being sure of 'the society' to which he referred, I replied, "Not yet, but now it matters even less!"

Together: Africa, The British Empire, Jamaica, New World Slavery and Britain make up our historical story. This story cannot be changed to suit the sensibilities of those who do not like parts of the whole. The entire story remains to be told to help improve community relationships because, for example, in a recent discussion of Britishness, very few people knew that the 'red areas' on an old map of the world depicted the British Empire; some thought the red areas were, "where it was hot"! At its simplest, our story says…we have a right to be here, in Britain.

Providentially, Reverend Nichol's 'mistake' of New World slavery has joined us together forever and cannot be dismissed by racial prejudice and the merciless self-interest shown by slave master William Adlam (1820) and his kind *(see Letter Home, p65)*. The enlightened comments and decree by Lord McEwan, in an Edinburgh court (May 2002), not only highlighted the wrongs of racism in a moral, lawful and therefore rightful society; they were also timely warnings to 'closet racists' and 'racists at large', as well as a severe punishment for a terrible crime against an ethnic person.

Racism is anti-creation, anti-country and illegal. That we have to imprison racists is regrettable. However, it is evident that some people derive status, power and pleasure from harming others, by 'sword or word'. It is sad that the law remains a primary defence against racism. In institutions, breaking of racial laws will not be excused by dismissive phrases such as, 'canteen culture', 'isolated case', 'indifference to race laws' or by the 'bad apple' analogy. Citizenship cannot be complete if rights, responsibilities and feelings of belonging are undermined by injustices such as racism.

Now, those who see the current concept of 'Institutional Racism' as a panacea, should note that racists in institutions, unlike racists on the street, tend to be 'closet racists' and are difficult to detect. They are masters of the racial aside which indicates personal problems of low esteem. The unfair job-selection policy of one such person was to turn down all candidates, if any candidate was of ethnic minority origin. This unacceptable practice not only denied jobs to qualified ethnic minority people, it prevented complaints of racism and circumvented the law. In a society where education fails to prevent or cure racism, the law cannot afford to fail. Institutions which have good race relations practice should be accredited to help remove backward indifference to the law.

It is baffling why even well-meaning people cannot understand that attempts to redress and remove colour prejudice are not special treatments, and that true equality will not be achieved until racist attitudes and ideologies that debilitate non-white people are banished from what we think and do. A white skin colour should not confer social advantages. A non-white skin colour is neither a disability nor an indicator of low potential. A short conversation overheard on a tube train may help to illustrate the importance of skin colour and prejudice in our society. Some time ago I boarded a tube train at Turnpike Lane in London after visiting my Mother who was very ill. Two old white men had just started a new topic in their conversation. "Herbie, whatever happened to your son?" "Ah, he went to Cambridge." "And did you ever change his name, Herbie?" "No, we never bothered because he got into a good law firm and now he is a judge, his foreign name doesn't matter anymore." Both men nodded, they were *system conscious*. For them, colour was not an issue but a foreign name was perceived to be a problem…a problem that could be managed by changing a name. Sadly, colour prejudice does not lend itself to such simple solutions. Fundamentally, skin colour is the important organ of the diversity of the Human Race, and its dishonouring by colour prejudice is mindless, irrational and unacceptable in a fair and just society. That colour (race) prejudice had to be made a crime to reduce the terrible abuse of non-white people, is one of the great tragedies of human history. It is not clear why we should have come to this but such tragedies tell us that although nature's future cannot be predicted, we can predict, to some degree, the consequences of the good or evil that we do.

System consciousness is an important feature of the education we require to live in any community. It is an essential component of citizenship. As a concept, it is easier to describe than define. For example it is that knowledge, which makes us aware that it is far wiser to leap into the dark with a torch than without!

System conscious education begins in the home and develops during schooling. Failure in this area of education limits the development of attitudes and skills required by individuals to respond appropriately to meet the interests of self and society which are important features of citizenship. Rules are essential ingredients of citizenship. System conscious education helps us to know and respect the rules. It also helps us to *play the game*. Role models have been proposed as an important learning strategy for children who have educational difficulties. Role models usually encourage imitation of life style, they are not substitutes for the education and skills required to meet social expectations. In the absence of effective strategies which promote educational development in different communities, the influence of the role model concept on poor-achievers is simplistic and is likely to be of limited educational value. Parents and teachers are the best role models for children.

System conscious education promotes social mobility and develops social potential. Social mobility enhances freedom and social potential allows opportunities to be taken. Therefore, any policy designed to develop learning and skills should include all aspects of system consciousness that help individuals to access the system and defend themselves against racist individuals and institutions. Effective control of racism in an institution is not about the role an ethnic minority person may play in that institution, it is often about the winks and nods and the illegal acts of group-cultures that deny rights and undermine fairness in institutions. Therefore, it is unlikely that institutional racism will be solved by faster promotions or better representation because it reflects historical prejudices, learnt in childhood, that defy decency and the law, and are difficult to change. The long term solution lies not with the stick of the 'race relations industry' but with the carrot of a balanced education at school.

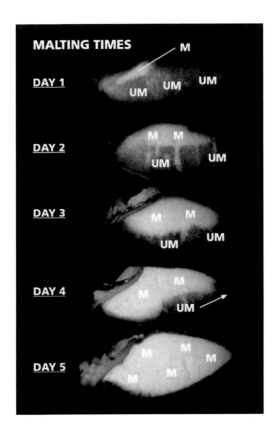

This photograph of mine shows one important feature of my early work in grain science and technology. Although regarded as 'controversial' by some, it confirms my early research that the pattern of enzymic breakdown (M) of food reserves in the germinated (malted) barley grain is asymmetric, not symmetric. Although I used the asymmetric concept to develop a new malting process (Abrasion, UK Patent no. 1264822; 56,57), the so called 'controversy' remains in some quarters...thankfully the science that makes good technology is blind to 'race and colour'.

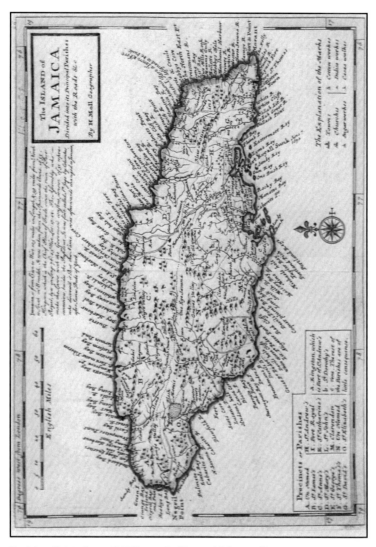

Re. Map. Original map (1729) is in the National Library of Jamaica.

Photo Gallery

Handcuff marked Hiatt

Handcuff marked 27 and FIELD

Regarding photos: These two heavy (3lbs) handcuffs of solid iron hang from a granite wall in a grand house where Henry Dundas, the lst Viscount Melville, lived in Scotland. The identities of these handcuffs are: Made by **Hiatt**, a company once based in Birmingham, England, that made 'slave ("Nigger") restraints' during British slavery. This piece of inhumanity weighs 1.5 lbs and was made to restrain, **FIELD**, chattel slave, **27**. This statement is a memorial to those for whom this disgraceful piece of inhumanity was made. Prime Minister Canning described Dundas as representing: "Pillage and Patronage" … to me, he had hands that took from slaves and gave it to slavers. The present attempt to re-write history and suggest that Henry Dundas was an abolitionist is a disrespectful insult to all the slaves that were killed during the period when Dundas' edict, that slavery should be 'gradually abolished', stopped William Wilberforce from abolishing the slave trade for 15 years (1792-1807). Those who site Henry Dundas' pleading in the Joseph Knight case, which essentially confirmed legal issues in the case, as the act of an abolitionist, insult chattel slaves, abolitionists and the descendants of slaves. To me, the Joseph Knight case (58) highlights a terrible social-legal hypocrisy…Knight was not a slave in England or Scotland but he would be **FIELD SLAVE 27** in Jamaica. These pictures remind me that: **Many prejudices of today are based on the cruelties of the past. If we know more and deal with the past, we can have a better future.**

Handcuff decoration...

FIGURES

Map of Jamaica: Black areas represent sites of cane sugar production, hatched areas represent coffee-growing areas (about 1805). In 1805 sugar production in Jamaica was worth about £600,000,000 to Britain ...in today's money (Api production, Jamaica, 1975). Slave population ca. 300,000...ca. £100 per 'best' slave.

Plantation in Jamaica: Slaves returning to the estate after a full day growing sugar cane and coffee (Hakwell, 1820).

Oakton Colonial House: In St. Andrews, Jamaica. Similar in design to East Street Colonial House, Kingston, Jamaica (1986).

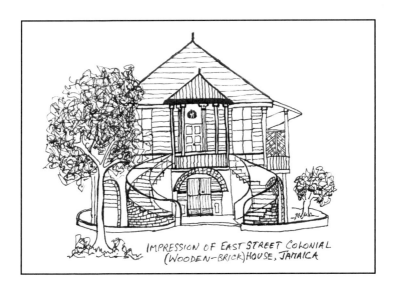

IMPRESSION OF EAST STREET COLONIAL (WOODEN-BRICK) HOUSE, JAMAICA

My Grandaunt: Auntie, on Sunday standing outside her Church, with her Bible (1958).

Aunt Mina, after Church (1935): Taken downtown (Orange Street) by Mr Morais.

My Grandaunt: Auntie, standing in our backyard at John Street, Allman Town, Jamaica (1958).

My Mother, brother and I in 1944, on Sunday after Church.
Photo taken downtown (Orange Street) By Morais, a local photographer.

Side entrance to North Street Congregational Church, Jamaica - now called
North Street United Church (built in 1837).

At my Aunts' house (post Allman Town) in Jamaica, after Church. From left to
right: Aunt Hilda, Uncle Ferdy, Aunt Laura in 1986.

At the side door of North Street Church, leading to my school and Princess Street (1986). From right, Aunt Kate and my cousin Liz. To my left Miss Rob (Robinson) my primary school headmistress.

My Mother is given flowers of appreciation by Mrs Mavis Stewart MBE (left) of the Association of Jamaicans in 2002.

Receiving a local carving from Mr Michael Karanja, Chief Executive of Kenya Breweries, for helping educational development in grain science in Kenya 1995.

Teaching and representing Britain during a export trade visit to China, 1999.

Professor Palmer: Chairman of the Scottish Section of The Institute of Brewing. Brewing and Distilling Conference, Aviemore 1991.

Professor Palmer: Showing British barley to overseas visitors at Heriot-Watt University, Edinburgh, Scotland. He has published extensively on Grain Science and was invited to write the foreword of the current *Encyclopedia on Grain Science (2004)*.

Valuable schoolboy cricketer

It was before the war that Islington last had a schoolboy representative in the All London Schools Cricket Team. This season, however, a boy of Shelburne Secondary School has played in it regularly. He is Godfrey Palmer, who at one time attended Kingston Senior School, Jamaica.

At the all-London trials in May, Palmer quickly impressed the selectors as a bowler of unusual ability and one selector commented that he had never before seen a boy who could turn the ball so viciously from the off. Palmer bowls his off breaks at above medium pace and with considerable accuracy. In addition, he is an aggressive bat, who can always be depended upon to go for the runs, and a sound fielder close to the wicket.

So far this season he has played in five games for London and against schools which included Winchester, Harrow and Eton. He has taken ten wickets for less than eight runs apiece. His best performance was against Eton when he bowled fifteen overs and took three wickets for nineteen runs.

An indication of Palmer's value to his team is that his side has only once been beaten. This includes matches for his school where, up to the present, he has taken eighteen wickets for 36 runs.

He has now been accepted as a member by the Winchmore Hill Cricket Club, so that he will continue to enjoy the game after he has left school.

[Photo by R. Barber, 3, Highbury Hill

Articles Published

by the author on Education, Britishness
and Citizenship, between 1969 and 2007,
as part of his voluntary work

WHERE CHILDREN STILL ARE SEEN AND NOT HEARD by Geoff Palmer

Published in the Times Educational Supplement, 20.3.70 to extend an earlier publication in the same Journal (15.8.1969), that ignorance of British West Indian culture is a major reason why many West Indian children fail in the educational system.

In Jamaica, children like myself started school at about seven years of age. The school would invariably be church-tied: the teachers were mighty and the British clergy all-mighty. The repetitive terror of the three Rs was only broken by long singing periods and compulsory Friday morning services in the adjoining church.

There I "singed" and I "songed" until I heard that my mother had scraped together enough money for me to join her in England. When I left Jamaica at the advanced age of 14 my education had progressed from my two-times to my 12-times table while my singing had rocketed from Three Blind Mice and Yes, Jesus Loves Me to the illustrious but mysterious heights of The Magnificat, Psalm 232, Who is Sylvia ?, Row Boys Row, and Loch Lomond.

Having only ever done arithmetic, to be asked at the end of an 11-day journey covering 5,000 miles to tackle rows of figures under the strange heading of "mathematics" was a paralysing encounter; after many failed tests I finally made it to Shelburne Road Secondary Modern School.

At school the behaviour of the teachers was rather perplexing at times. Lack of effort met with no verbal or physical retribution - the teacher merely passed on to the next boy. If there was any reading to be done, the teacher did it and there was also the additional luxury of no homework. To my relatives this was sheer folly but to me the teacher was like a kind relative.

In such a situation, one can easily see how a West Indian child can be inadvertently "passed over" academically. The apparent "softness" of the teacher is an ideal climate for the adjustment of the perplexed child. However, there are counter-pressures from the home, up to four hours' homework per day, and a parent might well find additional chores for a child who has no homework, as a deterrent against "laziness".

With continued criticism from home about his "dunceness", a child may become suspicious of his teacher, suspecting a deceitful plot to impede his academic progress. The teacher, often ignorant of the child's cultural and home experiences, may attribute the child's behaviour to maladjustment, low intelligence and language deficiencies.

Superimposed on this home-school conflict the child has the additional anxiety of being told that he doesn't speak English. Unlike the educated West Indian who knows the difference between Plantation English and Standard English, the West Indian immigrant cannot always see the difference. He becomes insecure and hurt when it is suggested that he doesn't speak English. His immediate reaction is one of confusion, suspicion and aggression to a statement which, if true, deprives him of the feeling of belonging that a language confers.

In schools where immigrant children are allowed to drift in increasing confusion, alarming and dangerous conclusions may be drawn from their performance of standard IQ tests. When I arrived in England I was slow to appreciate the purpose of "play bricks" and the different pronunciation of identical words often rendered them meaningless.

In difficult areas where local authorities have instituted good parent-school relations, pre-school centres, adequate primary schools and remedial language classes, West Indian children do as well as their English peers who also benefited from the improved facilities.

But some local educational authorities seem to have been somewhat slow to assist West Indian children and these unfortunate children must make, unassisted, the necessary adjustments between two deceptively similar cultures. It may be infinitely more difficult for a Jamaican child to unlearn Plantation English, with its deceptive similarities to Standard English, than for a Greek Cypriot child to grasp the differences between Greek and Standard English.

Often some parents don't help. The Jamaican immigrant philosophically accepts his low status and attributes it to a system which did not provide the educational opportunities he needed to be "somebody". He is therefore very concerned about the educational future of his children.

But with all their concern, many parents are now aware that some of their transferred cultural beliefs may be working against the academic performance of their children. For example, West Indian parents will buy large expensive encyclopaedias for their children, while refusing to buy more attractive annuals and popular readers, which they dismiss as "rubbish books". Curiosity is not always tolerated and an over-curious child may be punished for being "too inquisitive". The Victorian maxim that a child is supposed to be "seen and not heard" is still upheld. Play in the garden can be accepted but play in the house is often interpreted as "bone idleness" and chores are provided to correct this.

Fathers are too work-weary to take their sons on excursions; none the less there is strong resentment towards boys being part of an outside group or club, which many parents feel is the path to lawlessness. A child might have accepted this attitude in Jamaica, but seeing the activities of other children in England, the Jamaican child becomes resentful of its parents' apparent lack of interest in them. Some parents whom I have met complained that while teachers are prepared to provide running shoes and football boots for their children, they are not interested in giving them homework.

As a result of unfulfilled educational aspirations conflicts between parents and children tend to increase rather than die down after the child has left school. Some West Indian parents still consider children as a form of material and emotional insurance; any attempt of the child to assert itself as an independent working unit meets with strong disapproval, and interpreted as gross disobedience and ingratitude.

Continual nagging may drive a boy from his home and from the future security of his apprenticeship to the immediate monetary rewards of the factory. But boredom soon leads to irregular working habits, and eventually the boy joins a group of youths with similar frustrations. Confrontation with the law is the next step.

I once stood with a boy's mother in court and heard the magistrate deny legal aid on the grounds that "you coloured people have too many cars and houses". The boy comes to believe that he and his friends are the victims of white persecution, guiltless of any anti-social behaviour. At this stage institutional correction, just or unjust, is taken casually as confirmation of white prejudice.

For the sake of home and society, local education authorities youth employment officers and employers must make every effort to ensure that genuine ability in West Indian children is not overlooked. On the other hand teachers should be wary of making unrealistic promises about the child's future abilities merely to calm down anxious West Indian parents. This kind of thing only arouses parental hostility, both to the system and the child, when it leaves school without scholastic attainment.

If we are to prevent racism we must give political and financial support to people best qualified to teach and guide all young people. In the long run, only harm can come of a situation where immigration officers, local politicians and semi-officials continue to consider themselves experts on human behaviour and learning.

HANDSWORTH: CARIBBEAN BLACK COUNTRY
by Geoff Palmer

Published in the Times Educational Supplement, 16.6.72 to highlight some of the social complexities inherent in a British West Indian community.

If Brixton is little Jamaica then Handsworth, in Birmingham, is little Kingston. Direct Food Supplies of Soho Road does not sell Hovis: it sells hard-doe buns, sweet cup, goat, fish, skellion, pimento, grater (coconut) cake, cut (coconut) cake, renta yam, yellow yam, coco, ochra, green bananas, goat chops, garden eggs, chocho and bay rum. Behind the large plate-glass window, the Jamaican owner chops corned pig tails.

On the other side of the road is *The Elite*, an Asian shop. The window is decorated with rows of flaccid plucked chickens and unfamiliar little yellow balls. Then there are bird peppers, sweet potatoes, bags of corn meal, Oxford encyclopaedias and stocks of sugar cane, and bags of Joe Lyons fair cakes. A Jamaican woman enters the Asian shop and asks for a packet of Brooke Bond tea…"Just as good." "Not that tea," she says, "it's no damn good, my boy reckons that's the monkey tea!"

I follow her toward Thornhill Road. She goes into another Asian shop and I walk up Thornhill Road and enter (uninvited and unexpected) to the police station, which, according to the Handsworth report by Agustus John, "is one of the buildings most dreaded and most hated by black Handsworth". The building, which has obviously seen better days, is no more imposing than the Jamaican-occupied houses down the road. Indeed, the Rentokil quarters in nearby Grove Lane look the most prosperous in the immediate vicinity.

The hallway of the station is small, dull and quiet. To the right is the interview room and to the left a glass partition with a small "conversation" window. A white woman holds the hand of a dark* child, reports the disappearance of a purse and leaves. A Jamaican speaks in hushed tones about family matters. I tell the PC at the window that I would like to talk to someone who is involved with immigrants. He says that Sergeant Bradley, the CRC officer, is out, but will be back at 1pm.

I return at 1pm and am led into the interview room by Sergeant Bradley and another policeman who introduced himself as Bill. "I make frequent visits to the schools to answer questions about the attitudes of policemen to immigrants in Handsworth. Questions are invariably about police harassment, but it's usually about what their friends have told them," the CRC officer tells me. "Most of the kids have never been in trouble, and although the sessions are heated I am usually well received."

He maintains that as much as 60 per cent of the problems in which the police become embroiled are not really police matters and that there would be less ill-feeling in Handsworth if they were dealt with by qualified social bodies. "The schools should be involved in this aspect of community education because while English parents listen, most West Indian parents don't." But he believes that things are improving.

* used then to describe degree of black

"For example, the Handsworth Community Venture has bought a house to be run by a Jamaican, Mr. Vic Fennell, as an Advice Centre to prevent parents bringing their children to the station for advice. He explained the sensitivity of his job carefully, "You see, you raise your voice in anger because you're tired and the kid starts to manufacture hate and we're all in trouble".

PC Bill is an impassive Black Country man and has been a Handsworth policeman for 22 years. "Listen son, I know this area well. It was nice once...kippers and curtains...but it isn't now. It's not the immigrants' fault. The area has got old. Troublemakers come here and spend a few days and go away and tell a load of lies. I know more Jamaican parents than Gus John could ever dream of knowing. I visit their homes; I talk with them; they give me tea. Their boy misbehaves in the home: they say to him..."You do that again and out you go, boy." He does it again and there's no joking...out he goes. They complain to me that they throw their children out because of us, the police. I ask them: "How is this?" They say: "Back home we could give them a good hiding but here they threaten to put you, the police, on us. This has happened and it worries me because these are the kids the Black Power troublemakers are after."

He goes on: "There are no organized gangs in Handsworth. Jamaicans don't form gangs; they don't like rules and regulations. For example, there's a reggae party down the road and you tell them to turn down the noise as it's late and a neighbour has made a complaint: they'll suck their teeth and just ignore you...not because they want a fight but because they reckon that a 'little noise' isn't a crime. But we have to push the issue of the noise-complaint and in the end we have to arrest somebody.

"The responsible blacks who have lived a long time in Handsworth have come to terms with our way of life and are very conservative now. You tell me, where was Gus John when some of his friends picketed the station four weeks ago? Only 23 people arrived - out of a black community of thousands.

"You read about gangs in Handsworth and wrongful arrest...the kids that make trouble think they are right and we think they are wrong: mistakes happen but there's no organized law-breaking in Handsworth. The closest we got to an organized event was the abortive hot-air punch-up which was supposed to take place between the Handsworth Boys School (mostly black) and the Handsworth Grammar (mostly white) in Handsworth Park. We are not trained social workers, we are law-enforcement officers who have had to take on other duties which no one wants to do."

I leave the station with the intention of visiting some of the Jamaican-run pubs; of finding out more about the demonstration at the station and about some of the problems of black youth in Handsworth.

The Jamaican-run pubs in Handsworth are home from home institutions. After work the Jamaican men make their way to the pub to chat, drink beer and listen to non-stop reggae music. In the pub I visit the walls are lined with platted straw and bamboo. There is a composite picture of Jamaican scenery, a picture of John and Robert Kennedy with Martin Luther King between them and two African masks which the man beside me describes as, "being made right here in Birmingham". The publican is a shrewd

Jamaican ex-serviceman who sees trouble before it starts.

"Nice brotherman, cool it", is sufficient. As in the other Jamaican-run pubs or in clubs like the Beverly, his family helps behind the bar and they all wear a "Welcome" badge.

It is difficult not being a Jamaican in a Jamaican pub because the conversation invariably comes round to..."You remember Race Course"...or..."One night I was walking through Jones Town".

There are two Indian records to fifty Reggae or Tamla Motown records on the juke box but the Indians don't seem to mind. In another Jamaican-run pub down Soho Road, Jamaicans are seated in the Jamaica room and Indians are in the India room.

During a visit to the urinals a turbaned Indian tells me of the occasion he was on a bus in the city and a nice white woman asked him if he liked it in the city and how she was for integration and understanding of the races and when she got up to leave the bus she bade him goodbye and wished that his head would get better soon.   We both laugh and he goes back in the India room and I go to the Jamaica room to join my friend who tells me we have been invited to a party. Just as we are about to leave PC Bill and Sergeant Bradley come in and say hello to some of the Jamaicans and buy drinks: whether they are loved or not they are definitely not strangers in Handsworth.

A Jamaican birthday party in Handsworth is no different from the same event in London. The host is a tough beefy Jamaican and he is in charge of arrangements for his party. He lights the candles on the cake and says "his few words" and closes with a general rendering of the Lord's prayer. We all sing happy birthday to the well-dressed Jamaican girl at the end of the table and she blows out the candles and thanks us in a strong Birmingham accent.

The table is moved into the kitchen and the music starts again. After many whiskies and glasses of nutrament (an egg-flip-like drink designed for the Jamaican market), curry goat and pork, the guests drift away.

A small group sits and begins to talk. The host, who had recent business with the law, says: "I don't trust the British police... mind you I didn't trust the Jamaican ones either. As a black man I must sympathize with any black movement but although my association, WINA (West Indian National Association), asks all shades of militants to speak to us we do not let them interfere with our club. We have our own committee. We buy flats, put them right and let them cheaply to our people."

He explains: "The march on Thornhill Road police station against blatant police harassment failed because we were let down by immigrants who beforehand had pledged their support. Black people just don't want to be seen demonstrating outside the police station...they are afraid of victimization." "Afraid!" exclaimed another member of the group, "I'm not afraid, I have to go to work to pay my mortgage. Listen brother, why not get a lawyer to help fight your cause?"

Roy Pitters is a Jamaican youth worker and has lived in Birmingham for 23 years. Having heard his name mentioned in a conversation, I rang him and an hour later I was in his sittingroom. On the wall are two certificates, one of the National Association of Youth Clubs and the other The City of Birmingham Joint Training Committee for Youth Workers. "Up until 1967 there were only two black youth workers in Birmingham - much less Handsworth", he says, and adds that, "At that time many of our Jamaican youths carried knives and this resulted in the accidental stabbing of a youth in Handsworth Park. In the so-called Handsworth Report, Gus John intimates that because I stood outside youth clubs and begged my Jamaican boys to hand over their knives before entering, I betrayed them and am one of the most resented men in Handsworth today.

"Such nonsense doesn't worry me because while I was in Birmingham facing the knives and meeting church leaders and police officers in this front room about the question of my youths, Gus John was either in Grenada or Oxford doing theology. That kid died in my boy's arms and I didn't want any more deaths. It was a time of uncertainty and tension...we couldn't afford the luxury of another Notting Hill in Birmingham. When police brutality is suggested I am the first to protest about it...but I don't try and involve kids in an open confrontation with the police because I regard it as my responsibility to take the matter to the proper authorities which is invariably not the PC on the deck at Thornhill Road. What we want in Handsworth and other immigrant areas are black leaders who will live here and work here, explaining to their brothers the best action to take when difficulties arise...we don't want 5-day residents doing paid surveys.

"I have read that Jamaican kids are useless workers but I am a training instructor for the Amalgamated Power Engineers and if it were Monday I'd show you what the black apprentices can do."

In his report John dismisses current youth work in Handsworth but while I'd be the first to admit that we have a long way to go, some progress has definitely been made: in 1967 there were only two youth clubs for black kids. Today there is the Canterbury Cross with about 300-400 members, Rookery Road Club with 150-200 members, the new Oaklands Youth Centre costing £35,000, with about 300 members, where unemployed youth are attended to by the youth employment officer rather than at the depressing youth employment office. There is also the Newtown Centre at Lozells. The job situation is not rosey, the squeeze is tight in Handsworth and the problems of a black youth who wants to work are cumulative in their final effect.

He gives me a beer. "There are no gangs of black youths in Handsworth...the sooner white people realize that six black kids walking down the road or sitting in the park is not a gang, the better. Jamaicans like to improvise and the peripheral relations they form with each other do not satisfy the rigid rules of a gang group. Like any group they reassure each other when the "intellectuals", the police and their parents, reject them.

"People who 'drop in' on Handsworth don't realize that things like the employment of a full-time social worker at William Murdoch School and the fact that a black boy from that school got into Oxford is a tiny step in the right direction. Equally important is the fact that West Indians travel from Handsworth to Perry Barr to work their allotment, and have made a fantastic job of running many pubs in Handsworth. Blacks don't want patronage, they want an opportunity to explore their new environment.

"We want mothers to stay at home and bring up their children rather than hiving them off to dead-leg babyminders. To achieve this we have to give the immigrant the assurance that he will not be hounded out. Better and cheaper housing, job security, and well-publicized advice centres should provide this assurance. We want our brothers to stop talking and come to live here and help us."

When I arrived at the recently built New Town Centre, the West Indian boys and girls were paying their admission fee to enter what the poster on the door advertises as: New Town Centre Youth Clubs. "It all happens here. 8-14 years...6-8pm, 14-21 years... 7-10.30pm. Activities: Snooker, Table Tennis, Football, Dancing: Thursday, Every Thursday: Reggae - Disco 5p".

"The problem of youth in a deprived area is so vast that it cannot be put into neat academic packages," the warden, Peter Allen, tells me. "West Indians have no inherent sympathy with the way we, the English, do things. For example, the club rules say that the party ends at 10.30pm but they can see no harm in it going on until 1am. So when at first you say "stop" they just say "piss off". One cannot be taught to handle West Indian youth, one merely uses one's eyes and hopes that in time these kids will graduate from calling you: Man, Cock, Bossman, Guv, to *Peter*. This, in itself, is an achievement. To jostle them is an important form of physical contact or else the only contact you have with them is throwing them out. We don't have any Indian teenagers coming here...not formalized enough. However, during the week we have 60 to 70 unemployed Indians who come here to improve their English and to meet."

The West Indian Federation Association Youth Club presents a less optimistic scene. The front door opens on to Winson Green Prison and the inside of the building is in need of decoration. A new telephone lies on a chair. The front room is used for meetings and the large back room for parties. On a chair there is a leaflet calling for action to defeat racialism and unite against police harassment. In the back room an enthusiastic West Indian band, The Explosive Copper Coins band is rehearsing a song called "It's too late to say that you're sorry..." while two Jamaican youths sweep up the bottles, cans and cigarette butts. I asked them about the activities of the club. "The place is a bit rough but we like it here", one of them tells me, "because Mr. Hunt has Black Power ideas we don't get much cash. The police don't bother us much here but if we kids walk in a group and make a bit of noise they are likely to arrest you if you don't do as they say."

Back in Handsworth Park, I ask a Jamaican kid if he knows of any youth clubs in the area. He says, "Yes, the Canterbury Club." I ask him if he goes to the West Indian Federation: he says, "Yes." I ask him why and he says: "Down there, the sound (music) is better." A few steps further in the Park I ask a Jamaican parent what he thinks of the Federation and he says: "I had a decent Christian upbringing and a place in front of a prison is no place for decent kids to go."

If one is to find fault with the good intentions of those who have written about Handsworth (Gus John and John Lambure in The Handsworth Report: Jim Bergman and Bernard Coard in Race Today) attention must be focused on their over-obsession with the police bogy while ignoring the fact that "fluent Swahili" is no substitute for the "detested white-orientated education".

Deprived youth, with no possibility of area mobility, not only require continuity of teaching, but in school they also require continuity and confidence in youth leadership. They need, as Dr. Robert Holman of the Handsworth Adventure Play says, detached youth workers in the Handsworth scene. They want people who will live locally and involve the kids in activities which are beneficial to themselves and the community in which they live. Qualified blacks must go to the "Black Country" to lead.

Postscript 2004: On Saturday the 10th of July 2004 I was given the honour to present the prizes and give a talk on science as a career to the Ishango Science Club Ltd., in Birmingham. The large classroom was full of local black children and their parents. In attendance were volunteer teachers, staff, the Chair – Monica Coke, the Project Manager – Karen Gardiner and Lloyd Blake of the Institute of Jamaica Nationals, Birmingham. This scheme is sponsored by the Birmingham Core Skills Development Partnership and is a successful development, which shows that the difficulties of 1972 were not insurmountable and are being overcome by committed people and institutions. This initiative is a workable model as regards the Science, Engineering and Technology (S. E. T.) scheme, which could be introduced in areas where children need additional educational support.

FOOD FOR THOUGHT IN MULTICULTURAL BRITAIN by Geoff Palmer

Published in the Sunday Express, 25.6.2000 to illustrate that foods from the countries of non-white people (ethnic foods) are an important part of multicultralism in Britain.

Variety is the spice of life, and you need look no further than the haggis for proof of that. For decades, people, inside and outside government have struggled to bring home the concept of a multicultural society. In the Sixties, people talked of New York being a melting pot where the world's nations rubbed shoulders, making it the world's most exciting city.

And maybe the analogy wasn't far wrong for Britain too. Tangerines, tomatoes, chocolate, coffee, sugar, tea, cornflakes, rhubarb, cucumbers, onions, and olive oil, are some of the foods which we in Britain eat every day and are regarded as staples of the British diet. But they are of ethnic origin.

An important feature of any society is that the people in it should have mutual respect for each other's contribution. What more important contribution is there than food? Food which has sustained the people of this society.

The basic mediaeval Scottish diet, although often cited as being healthy, was extremely uninteresting, comprising mainly of soups, purees, beet leaves, cabbage, onions, turnips, leeks and, for the fortunate, salted beef, pork or fish. But that began to change in the 12th century when the package tourists of their day, the Crusaders, brought back sugar from the Middle East.

The history of the British Empire for over three hundred years has been one of securing and maintaining our food supply from the colonies. During the 17th Century, the English fought the Portuguese to secure spices such as cloves, nutmeg and cinnamon to improve the British diet.

Between 1700-1800, the British diet, because of colonisation, had changed dramatically to include tea, coffee, chocolate, potatoes, tomatoes and spices. Economically, and in terms of diet, sugar was regarded as the most important food product by the British. It came primarily from the West Indies colonies. Some of the most important naval battles fought by the British were fought in defence of West Indian islands that had a large Scottish population at the time.

One of the most vital of these was fought against the French in 1782 by Admiral Lord Rodney, which came to be known as the Battle of All Saints or the Battle of the Glorious Twelfth. The significance of this battle can be measured against the fact that the British had "surrendered" to the Americans in 1781, while one of the largest fleets ever put to sea by Britain was off the coast of Florida to fight the French, to protect Jamaica and maintain British dominance in the production of sugar, rum, coffee and spices.

The historical importance of this battle can also be deduced from the knowledge that Rodney had 36 warships and Nelson, at Trafalgar, only had 29. Robert Burns deemed it important enough to write a song about the British victory.

Instead of a song, boys, I'll give you a toast;
Here to the memory of those on the Twelfth we lost;
That we lost, did I say, nay, by heaven that we found,
For their fame it shall last while the world go round.

The benefits of these wars resulted in the development of a supply of cheap food such as sugar, spices, coffee, tea and chocolate from the West Indies and Asia.

Britain's ports grew rich on this trade. Shop owners, such as Thomas Lipton, created the forerunners of our supermarkets. It is curious that our present supermarkets provide one of the few places where the white population is brought into contact with the products of British colonialism without being aware of it. It is also important to note the role, culturally and economically, Indian and Chinese restaurants play in British life.

The Government has emphasised the school curriculum should reflect the multicultural nature of our society. However, there has been little progress. One reason is ignorance of the contribution the colonies have made to this country. It is from this seed of ignorance the monster, racism, continues to grow, spread and divide the human race.

As a Jamaican immigrant who teaches brewing, it gives me pleasure to know Red Stripe and Cobra are among our most successful lagers and they are brewed in the UK by British students whom I have had the privilege to teach.

This is the true nature of the multicultural melting pot. The supermarket shelf is the place where multiculturalism cannot be denied. What has been ignored in the supermarket should become an important part of education.

PUNISHED FOR BEING JAMAICAN by Geoff Palmer

Published in the Edinburgh Evening News, 25.1.03 in response to the visa restrictions imposed on Jamaica in 2003.

Punish the guilty, not the people of Jamaica. Punish the guilty that evade immigration rules, trade in drugs and carry and use guns illegally. But why punish the people of Jamaica for the actions of criminals - some born in Jamaica others born in Britain?

Law-abiding Jamaicans are dismayed that the long 348 years of links between Jamaica and Britain could have been damaged by the actions of people over whom they had no control.

The causes of this criminality are various. Some say that they come from the poverty of Jamaica and the absence of a sense of belonging in Britain. Notwithstanding, the law must be upheld and the people of Jamaica are fully aware of this. That they should have to pay the price of visa restrictions for crimes committed in Britain has damaged the well-being of a proud people that have had to survive on a small, poor island that was, during slavery, the economic jewel in the crown of the British Empire. Kingston Docks in Glasgow and Inveresk Lodge, Inveresk (near Edinburgh) came from this abundance.

During rapid immigration between 1950-1960, Jamaicans worked in jobs that no-one else wanted. These jobs were vital for the post-war recovery of Britain. And most recently, senior nurses have been recruited from Jamaica to help run our hospitals.

However, from the 9th January, 2003, Jamaicans travelling to the

UK will require a visa for the first time in nearly 350 years. The governments of Jamaica and Britain have been in negotiations for two years about ways of dealing with the entry of Jamaicans into Britain. Unfortunately, the timing of the British government to impose visa restrictions on Jamaicans has linked the visa issue to the terrible and tragic killing of Charlene Ellis and Latisha Shakespeare in Birmingham on 2nd January, 2003. Jamaicans are distressed by this perception because those involved in this evil crime are likely to have been British citizens, born in Britain. That many people referred to this tragic local crime as a "black-on-black" crime was disgraceful. The racial undertone of this mindless definition is that "black-on-white" crimes and "white-on-white" or "white and black" crimes are more acceptable forms of criminality.

The causes of the Birmingham tragedy are very complex. The crime appears to have been a local act of illegal possession and use of guns. The growing similarity between the use of guns in deprived communities in Britain, like America, reflects the misguided view that guns and knives offer "personal protection" in a violent environment. This kind of social separation tends to exclude the police. In consequence, the support the police needs to solve many local crimes is often withheld. Even community leaders find it difficult to establish lasting social connection with disaffected young people...this is a bio-social problem, not an affliction exported from Jamaica.

That rap music initiates violence is a view based on very little evidence. Beat music has always been associated with current trends in youth violence. The evidence that shows that youth violence is reduced in the absence of beat music does not seem to be available. Until this evidence is available it would be unwise to make such statements which have a ring of anti-black music about them. Jamaican music is a valuable contribution to world music but surely this is hardly a good reason for imposing a visa sanction on its population.

Some of the more serious reasons for imposing visa sanctions on Jamaicans are that six per cent of Jamaican visitors (3,340 people) were refused entry in 2001 and more than 1,000 Jamaicans (mainly children) failed to return to Jamaica in 2002. In 2002, 1,283 Jamaicans were refused entry, a significantly smaller number than the 3,340 of 2001, suggesting that control systems were improving and that the justification of the visa sanction is questionable.

Linked to these immigration issues is the view that many visitors from Jamaica transport drugs to Britain. Although the perception is that Jamaicans are primary transporters of drugs, the Home Office figures published in December, 2002 stated that, of the 40 to 50 tonnes of cocaine shipped to Britain, about 15 per cent came in by air transport worldwide...Jamaica is regrettably a part of this 15%. However, the bulk of the disgracefully large quantity of cocaine that comes into Britain is shipped from various continental countries, many of which have no visa restrictions for entry into Britain.

The vast majority of Jamaicans in Britain are hard-working members of the community and are proud of their long historical links with Britain. First language is an important aspect of culture... the only language of Jamaicans is English, they are treated like social outsiders. At the recent Annual Dinner of the Birmingham based Institute of Jamaican Nationals, that was held at the Aston Villa Football Stadium, I was delighted to have been asked to propose the toast to the Institute and its 555 guests. The event was peaceful and dignified and the Queen was toasted respectfully in the usual manner. An old Jamaican man reminded me after the dinner that Robert Burns' favourite country, after Scotland, was Jamaica. At a meeting of the Leeds Jamaican Association and the London Jamaican Association I encountered the same confidence and Britishness. These aspects of social belonging are sadly missing from the lives of many Jamaican children born in Britain who are descended from black African and white British people yet look only to Africa for identity rather than to Britain, where their heritage through history, name and ancestors is more traceable. Citizenship comes out of a sense of belonging that is based on the belief that social responsibility is the price of equal rights. If rights are not equal or are perceived as not equal, it is difficult to teach social responsibilities. Our history and genes give us a right to be here and this cannot be dismissed or changed by words or deeds from any quarter.

The Home Secretary's view that the imposition of a visa will speed up the passage of "genuine passengers" may indeed be correct. But the possession of a visa will not be a guarantee that the individual carrying it will not have criminal intentions. In fact, the 36 pounds (about 3,600 Jamaican dollars) required for the purchase of the visa and the "expensive" bureaucracy that will be required to secure a visa will increase the percentage of people who may be forced to carry drugs in exchange for a visa.

The main resource left to Jamaicans, after British colonial rule that lasted from 1655 to 1962, is their pride. It is unpardonable that this pride should have been attacked and damaged by the evil actions of those who trade in drugs and guns. The government and the people of Jamaica would never condone such senseless crimes.

It is understandable that the British Government must act to protect law and order in Britain. All Jamaicans understand this position. However, the distress they now endure is the unjust public perception that the visa imposition is linked to the criminal events that took the innocent lives of two promising young ladies on the streets of Birmingham.

However, below the surface of this distress is the optimistic and essentially Christian view that this visa decision will be reversed in the future when it is realized, through education, that the population of Jamaica are not outsiders and not involved in law-breaking in Britain. Jamaicans will work to remove the visa restrictions. At present, they are also working to save their sugar industry from damage proposed by unenlightened sugar policies of the European Commission. Such damage to cane sugar will increase deprivation that started in slavery when Jamaica produced as much as half the world's sugar for Britain. For a small, poor country such as Jamaica to succeed in reducing crimes driven from outside the island, it requires *self-helping* support from Britain to save the residue of a sugar industry that did more than its share to build and sustain an Empire that was British.

EDUCATION, RACE AND CITIZENSHIP
by Geoff Palmer

Written in 2004. Taken from a lecture given at a conference on Citizenship at Edinburgh University, organised by The School of Divinity, Centre for Theology and Public Issues, Edinburgh University, 2003.

Racial tolerance and good citizenship are two of the primary aims of any civilised society. Two institutions to which this important responsibility has been allocated are: Education and the Law. It is therefore evident that if education fails, the law cannot afford to fail. That we, in the United Kingdom have had to pass race relation laws to protect the rights of people of different races, is an indication that education has not managed to convince us that racial prejudice is unfair and wrong. Indeed, the so-called philosophical concepts of an adviser to the Home Secretary propose that, it makes good sense for an employer not to employ black workers if his or her customers will not deal with black people. Such a concept is irrational and absurd in view of the law and the aim to develop good citizenship, where self-interest and greed do not limit rights and justice. However, I still believe that real and lasting improvements in race relations will come from appropriate educational initiatives.

Educational initiatives that work are those which develop admiration and respect for the rights of all the people of our community. Culture embodies customs and practices of different human beings. There is no consistent evidence, that people of different cultures cannot be Citizens of the same community, if a sense of belonging is promoted. The word "race" is divisive and has been used to put people in a social pecking order. Therefore, the continued usage of the word race, when we mean ethnic, reinforces prejudices that state that different races exist.

Our languages and our histories influence our ideologies. For example, there are a large number of people who believe that only white people can be Scottish, English, Irish, Welsh or British. The reason for this belief is difficult to identify but many of our racial prejudices stem from such a view. The word "race" has no clear meaning and carries with it beliefs of social and genetic differences which embody superiority and inferiority. However, the following examples show how the word race can convey differences between people which, on the most superficial examination, do not make sense. We use the words Human Race to convey universal humanity. However, we glibly refer to ourselves as members of, the Scottish race, the English race, the French race or the German race. However, we do not regard a Nigerian as belonging to the Nigerian race or a Kenyan as belonging to the Kenyan race or a Jamaican as belonging to the Jamaican race. Curiously, we tend to regard all black people as belonging to the black race, without having equivalent national and cultural distinctiveness.

The word race exaggerates the importance of skin colour and features but underrates the overriding uniformity of the biological function of humanity. Racism is therefore a product of the human mind...it is based on an evil that deludes but seems right to people who do not know the difference between cultural difference and genetic difference. Indeed, we get some of our fear of the "foreigner" from Gibbons who sold the yarn that if the barbarians can destroy Rome, other foreigners can destroy Britain. Since the British population consists of many foreigners, Gibbons' view does not make sense but this is the essence of racism...what is believed does not make sense.

Hume, our great philosopher, also had a problem with the concept of race. He, with all his mighty intellect, could not accept that because Africans have not built anything like the Castle, they must be inferior to white men. It did not seem to cross Hume's great mind that geography, need and circumstances play a major part in human activity. What is more astonishing than Hume's misunderstanding is that his erroneous view is still held today to the detriment of black people.

One should not be able to turn a "prejudice" into a "fact" but, to justify racism, various scientists have tried to produce evidence that differences in the performance of different "races" in psychology (intelligence) tests are based on genetic differences. The prejudice here is that different races have had different historical experience and no decent researcher would compare the performance of two rats in a test that have had distinctly different histories. Curiously, what would be regarded as unfair and unscientific for rats is regarded as quite suitable for human beings, even though the results of such tests could deny people their due respect and rights.

I see no reason why black or white foreigners cannot be British citizens. White foreigners seem to progress faster in the system than black foreigners. Indeed, many so-called black foreigners, like myself, are long standing members of the British Empire. Jamaica became part of the Empire in 1655 and has derived its language and culture primarily from its Britishness. Many Jamaicans are descended from black and white people. The white ancestors of many Jamaicans are Scottish, many of whom were slave masters. Britishness was a political concept of a world of different people living on the "red areas" of the map of the world. It has nothing to do with colour and race. That to be British...is to be white, is historical nonsense.

After over three hundred years of Britishness, it is problematic that we can subject a Jamaican or any other people of the old British Empire to a British citizen test. There is an inherent injustice in this. That people of the old British Empire should have to pay very high fees to enter our universities does not seem right. That black people, of one of the oldest sections of the British Empire, should be deprived of social rights and be subjected to the indignity of having the right to call themselves black, put out to consultation by civil servants, is an impudent attack on the identity of creation and a large backward step for race relations in Britain. *My colour is me.* It will not be bartered, bought or sold again. Overt racism or the covert racism of the "wink and nod" racist should not be tolerated, from any group or from any quarter.

Recently it has been proposed that multiculturalism is a limitation to the development of Britishness and should be discontinued as a concept. This is incorrect. Multiculturalism teaches social co-existence: Britishness embodies political belonging. Both concepts complement each other to produce citizens with equal rights and responsibilities. The greatest limitation to the development of citizenship is not multiculturalism, it is the word race. It is divisive in every context in which it is used and should be abolished.

Citizenship is not about which team one cheers for in sport, it is about a sense of belonging that comes from the feeling that rights are equal. Many Scottish and Welsh people do not cheer for England in sport but are not disloyal to the country...

System consciousness is a term I use to describe one of the important out-comes of education. Without it, it is difficult to function successfully in any society. To produce good citizens, we must not only give people a sense of belonging, we must also ensure that they develop the system consciousness they need to function equally in the society.

FREEDOM COLOUR PREJUDICE
by Geoff Palmer

First appeared in Edinburgh and Lothian Racial Equality Council's Newsletter, December 2006

"My colour is me..." says the poet proudly (Edinburgh and Lothians Racial Equality Council's 35th Anniversary magazine, 2006). Here he tells us that skin colour is a primary part of his slave heritage and freedom: to write it out of documents is a gross insult to natural identity.

The year 2007 will be the 200th anniversary of the abolition of the British Slave Trade. School children to Governments of the United Kingdom are working to commemorate the ending of the purchase/capture and transport of millions of black people, from Africa to areas of the New World such as the West Indies and America.

This short piece is not about the abolition of the slave trade or slavery; it is about the current attempt to remove the word "black" from official documents such as census forms. As a descendant of black Jamaican slaves, I find this intention offensive to my history. I cannot speak for all the descendants of New World slaves but my experience indicates that we honour the skin colour of our slave ancestors and do not want the right to describe ourselves as black taken away by people who do not understand, share or respect our historical experience.

That the eloquence to the biblical phrase, "black but comely", was reworked by racists to create the perception of inferiority and justify enslavement, was a terrible evil. The work of DuBois, Marcus Garvey, Senghor, Biko and others returned the skin colour black to its proper place as a dignified description of a large section of the human race. Out of this work came the renaissance concept of "Black Consciousness"...a concept that has made it possible for a black skin colour to be worn with dignity by anyone that carries the genes of black people. In this regard, black consciousness is about dignity in self, irrespective of the views of others. That anyone would wish to deny the significance of this re-gained dignity of black people reflects ignorance at its worst.

Any attempt to remove the rights of people to describe them as they see themselves is an unacceptable denial of human rights. It is well known that the first step in taking away the freedom of any group of people is the removal of their identity. This pointless attempt to deny me the right to call myself black is an assault on my freedom. I will not accept this. To propose that I should call myself African Jamaican/Caribbean, instead of Black Jamaican/Caribbean is as ridiculous as, one or two Europeans forcing white Americans, whose white ancestors have lived in America for centuries, to call themselves European Americans. Although I respect African people and people who are conveniently black, I will not be a victim of such bad reasoning. In this I expect protection from my government.

Logically, the removal of the colour black, from forms, should also result in the removal of the colour white. Both these changes will require the consent of both races as is clear from the Race Relations Amendment Act 2000. This has not yet been done but must be done to protect the freedom of both races. In addition, the removal of skin colour will make it impossible to monitor racism that is linked to colour. Also, there will be the dangerous deception that, in time, the present significant level of racism towards black people will disappear statistically if the black population is subsumed into a large minority ethnic population. For the sake of peace and progress in our society this must not be allowed to happen.

To try and explain away the word "Black" as an all embracing political concept of "non-whiteness", is unwise, unsound, wrong and disrespectful to black people, descended from a slavery that has been described as "the most profitable evil the world has known". I value the dignity my colour gives me. Racial abuse using the word black will increase if the dignity of the word is slipped under the political carpet. This will cause even greater discomfort to those who do not want to be called black. Such perverse outcomes usually emerge from decisions based on lopsided lobbying and scaremongering, rather than on sound scientific evidence.

Choice is an important part of what we call freedom. That some people do not want to tick skin colour on forms should not deny me the human right of registering my identity as a black person.

THE 200 YEAR COMMEMORATION OF THE ABOLITION OF THE BRITISH SLAVE TRADE IN THE WEST INDIES: 1807-2007

FREEDOM WALK: From Musselburgh High Street to Inveresk Lodge.

The route re-enacts the journey taken by the Jamaican ex-slave Robert Wedderburn in 1795 to see his Scottish father, the ex-slave master James Wedderburn. Robert Wedderburn was born into British slavery in Jamaica in 1762. He was the son of the white slave master, James Wedderburn and a black slave woman, Rosanna.

James Wedderburn, a Scot, went to Jamaica in 1746. He became a notorious slave master and in 1773 returned to Scotland and bought Inveresk Lodge with the money he made, after 27 years in Jamaica, as a slave master. He married well and his Scottish family benefited from his exploits in Jamaica.

In contrast, his slave-son, Robert Wedderburn was forgotten until 1795 when, after gaining his freedom, he travelled from London to Scotland and from Musselburgh to Inveresk Lodge to find his father, James Wedderburn.

James Wedderburn did not allow Robert Wedderburn to enter his house and drove him away with the insulting gift of a "cracked sixpence". Robert Wedderburn (also known as Reverend Robert Wedderburn) returned to London and for the rest of his life, worked as a radical anti-slavery activist. His great rage against chattel slavery in the British West Indies was well known to other abolitionists such as William Wilberforce.

Robert Wedderburn preached and wrote with great force that such slavery was against God, anti-Christian and uncivilised. Thankfully, the British slave trade (abolished 1807) and British slavery (abolished 1834) ended before Robert Wedderburn died in London in 1835.

This commemorative walk of freedom symbolises the hope, the rejection, the hard work and the triumph of a human being who bravely preached that slavery is a grotesque evil that should not be practiced or tolerated by anyone, anywhere.

In 2003, Lord (Professor) Bill Wedderburn (a descendant of Robert Wedderburn) and his wife visited Inveresk Lodge. They visited the house and walked around the beautiful gardens, now owned by the National Trust for Scotland. As we walk through the silence of the garden our thoughts should be on Robert Wedderburn, the ex-slave, who turned his rejection from this house, his father's house, into a quest for freedom...a freedom that brings us together today to celebrate our common humanity.

Material taken from: The Enlightenment-Citizen of Britishness,
Geoff Palmer, Henry Publishing, 2003.

The National Trust for Scotland acknowledges the kind permission of Geoff Palmer in allowing us to reproduce this history.

BURNS: JAMAICA STREET TO OSWALD TOWER

There are two old streets in Glasgow called Jamaica Street (1763) and Oswald Street (1817). Jamaica Street and Oswald Street run closely together locally and historically. There is also a large stained glass window in Glasgow Cathedral which commemorates the 'generosity' of the Oswald family who were slave owners in countries such as Jamaica. Another stained-glass window defends this slavery as a "civilising mission". Although the Oswald family had a unique burial plot inside the Cathedral, Richard Oswald (1705-1784), who bulk-sold slaves and had slave plantations in Jamaica, is buried in the family vault of his own church, St Quivox. St Quivox, in Ayr, was part of the Auchencruive Estate Richard Oswald bought in 1764 with money earned from British chattel slavery. He also built a Family Gallery in his church and donated communion cups which are still in use today. That black chattel slave women were mothers of the children of white slave masters attested to a common humanity not reflected in the disconnect of Oswald and other slave owners such as John Gladstone (1764-1851) who enslaved and prayed, in their own churches. Historically, it was this disconnect, promoted officially by governments and slave owners, that made New World slavery unique as the most profitable evil our world has known.

Although the Oswald family members were well known as successful merchants, the life of Richard Oswald shows that chattel slavery was an official money-making business. He was born in 1705, his father was the Reverend George Oswald of Dunnet, Caithness. Like many young men, he worked as a trainee in the counting house of Old Glasgow Green in Glasgow, buying and selling slave-grown products. Tobacco, sugar and coffee were major products of British slavery that came to British ports and cities such as Glasgow.

By 1745, Richard Oswald made rapid progress in the mercantile business in Glasgow and moved to London and then Jamaica to exploit the opportunities of buying, selling and owning slaves. It was not uncommon for Scottish slave owners to marry widows or women who owned slave plantations left to them by deceased husbands or fathers. While in Jamaica, Richard Oswald was introduced to Mary Ramsay by Dr. Alexander Grant of Dalvey who had married the daughter of slave master Robert Cootes. Mary Ramsay owned slave plantations left to her by her deceased father. Richard Oswald was previously married to Agnes Barr in Scotland. However, he married Mary Ramsay in London at St Martins-in-the Field, in November 1750. He was 45 years of age and she was 31 years of age. Similarly, at that time, Sir Archibald Grant (1696-1778), of the Monymusk estate in Scotland and the owner of the Monymusk slave plantation in Jamaica, married in 1755 the widow of James Callander. She had inherited her deceased husband's slave plantations before her marriage to Archibald Grant.

In 1752, Richard Oswald and the Grant family became partners in the ownership of a company that bought Bance Island, an island close to the coast of Sierra Leone. Bance Island was used to bulk-sell slaves for transport across the Atlantic to slavery in the Caribbean. In addition to his slavery business, Richard Oswald sold 'bread' to the military during the Seven Years War (1756-1763), when the British army was protecting his interest by quelling slave rebellions, such as the Tacky rebellion in Jamaica in 1760, for which Tacky was hanged. Oswald's commercial greed caused Robert Burns (1759-1796) to damn him as a "Plunderer of Armies" in his vitriolic anti-Oswald poem, Ode, sacred to the memory of Mrs. Oswald of Auchencruive (1789).

After setting up Bance island's slave-selling supermarket in 1752, Oswald continued to develop his ruthless ambitions of being as rich and powerful as possible. Using his London, Jamaica and America links he encouraged James Grant, the British governor of East Florida to give generous land grants to the English slavery planter Francis Levett, enabling him to grow vast crops of rice and indigo. He was also involved in the development of Nova Scotia by petitioning the Board of Trade and Plantations, recommending those who should be given profit-making opportunities. Oswald's Nova Scotia became the place to where Jamaican Maroons were transported in 1795, to die in the cold or be sent to Sierra Leone, after their final war against the British army under the command of Lord Balcarres (see Balcarres Street, Edinburgh). Oswald also engaged John Levett, the brother of Francis Levett, to sell 'wigs' for him in Calcutta. Richard Oswald's extensive network was designed to increase the wealth and power of his slavery business.

The last three years of Richard Oswald's life (1781-1784) are important historically because they explain Robert Burns' 'unsacred' damnation of the dishonest wealth of the Oswalds in his poem, "Ode, sacred to the memory of Mrs Oswald of Auchencruive".

In 1781 Richard Oswald lobbied successfully for the release of Henry Laurens, the South Carolina slave owner. Laurens was captured by the Royal Navy when he was returning from negotiating Dutch support for the American War of Independence. In 1781, Don Francisco Saavedra said that the political aim of France and Spain, "Was to conquer Jamaica, the centre of the wealth and power of Great Britain in that part of the world." At that time, Jamaica was more valuable to the British economy than the thirteen Colonies of America. The First objective of the French and the Spanish was to assist in the defeat of the British at Yorktown in October 1781. This was effected by Admiral de Grasse after planning with Saavedra. Admiral Francois Joseph Paul de Grasse commanded the French Fleet which prevented the British Squadron from assisting Admiral Cornwallis (see Cornwallis Street, Edinburgh, next to Rodney Street) who was defeated by the Americans, commanded by George Washington. Buoyed up by this 'defeat' of the British in a half-hearted Kith and Kin war of independence, Admiral de Grasse sailed to join his Spanish allies to conquer Jamaica the following April of 1782.

However, to defend the greater value of Jamaica with its population of nearly 300,000 unpaid slaves, Britain sent down its Naval "A-team" Fleet, commanded by Admiral George Rodney (see Rodney Street, Edinburgh) and Admiral Samuel Hood (see famous Battleship). Using novel faster copper-bottomed ships and using new strategies such as "breaking the line", Rodney and Hood captured de Grasse and inflicted a devastating defeat on the Fleet he commanded. The dead and the wounded from this fight for the financial income from slavery in Jamaica, at the Battle of the Glorious 12th of April 1782 (also called the Battle of the Saintes) are recorded as following: The British, 243 dead and 816 wounded. The French, 3,000 dead or wounded and 5,000 captured. To understand the impact of the past, all known sections of the history of that past, such those of chattel slavery, should be taught together. Inclusive facts, such as the truth about our involvement in chattel slavery will produce better 'race' relations than the fiction of forgetfulness invented by historians to absolve and please.

Richard Oswald, who owned slaves in Jamaica, was aware of the economic significance of the Battle of the Saintes; so was Robert Burns who referred to it in 1793 in a toast... "Here's to the memory of those on the twelfth that we lost", to attest to his Britishness although he wrote, Scots wa hae, in the same year. Here, Burns showed a system conscious mix of diplomacy and defiance at a time when he worked as an excise officer and Britain was at war with a socially reformed France and, in place, were the sedition laws of Henry Dundas (who delayed Wilberforce's efforts to abolish the Slave Trade (1807) for about 15 years) and William Pitt (who died (1806) regretting that he did not do more to abolish British slavery).

Richard Oswald's extensive links with the establishment and business people of slavery caused Lord Shelburne to select him as Britain's Peace Commissioner to assist in the re-allocation of land and countries, after the Battle of the Saintes in 1782. For example, he helped to set the border between the United States and Canada which still exists today. The French were given Tobago and Senegal but were saddled with a large debt. Spain was given a part of Florida and Britain consolidated its hold on Gibraltar and elsewhere in the Caribbean. On the 25th July 1782, the preliminary articles of the Treaty of Paris were signed by Oswald for Britain. Later, on the 30th November 1782, his fellow Commissioners, John

Adams (future President of the United States), Benjamin Franklin (famous scientist and statesman), John Jay and Henry Laurens (slave owning partner of Oswald) signed for a free United States.

In 1783, after his spell as British Peace Commissioner when the Treaty was ratified, Richard Oswald returned to the grandeur of Auchencruive House and its Tower, in Ayr, built by Robert Adam, which he had bought in 1764. Oswald died in 1784 leaving over £400,000,000 in today's money, made primarily from the profitable evil called chattel slavery.

The wealth of the Oswald family was well known and resentment of this wealth is set down clearly in Robert Burns' poem, Ode, sacred to the memory of Mrs Oswald of Auchencruvie (1789). The poem came out of the route which the funeral procession of Mrs. Oswald (Mary Ramsay) took in 1789. Burns was ejected from his residence at the Inn in Sanquhar, on a cold, wild wet and windy January night, to an alternative residence 12 miles way in New Cumnock, to accommodate the funeral party of Richard Oswald's wife. Burns' described the deceased Mrs Oswald's as, "Laden with unhonour'd years, Noosing with care a bursting purse", and the unworthy recipient of an annuity of, "Ten thousand of glittering pounds a-year?" Many millions in today's money. Burns then equated her avarice to:

"Hands that took but never gave.

Keeper of Mannon's iron chest, Lo, there she goes, unpitied and unblest,

She goes, but not to realms of everlasting rest!"

Burns' poem is not only a powerful description of avarice and greed, it is an important historical record of the dishonour of the wealth that slavery produced, a slavery which he nearly joined as a "slave driver" in 1786 ("Will Ye Go to the Indies my Mary") because it was believed then that chattel slavery was an officially acceptable way of bettering oneself. Oswald's' wealth in Auchencruive was only a few miles away from where Burns lived. Burns' dislike of the Oswalds may also have been fuelled by his knowledge of the origins of the slavery-derived wealth of William Cunninghame, the slaver, whose 1778 Glasgow mansion is now the Gallery of Modern Art. He would have also been aware of the slavery-derived wealth of the Glassfords and Robertsons, the Wedderburns and Selkirks, the Buchanans and Spiers and the Grants and Stirlings. As prejudice is the worst part of humanity, redemption is the best part and Burns redeemed himself in 1792 and 1795 when he wrote respectively," The Slave's Lament" (1792) and "A Man's A Man For A' That" (1795). These poems remind us of Sir Donald Burns Sangster (1911-1967). His Scottish ancestry in Jamaica began during slavery the year Burns wrote "The Slave's Lament" (1792). It started from John Sangster, born in Banff and Bessy of Jamaica. "For A' That", Donald Burns Sangster became the second Prime Minister of Jamaica in 1967.

During a recent interview on Radio Scotland, a lecturer in American history said that the violence in the new Roots series of 2017 was increased to show the true violence of slavery. In contrast, I said that knowing that, the grand building that contains Glasgow's Gallery of Modern Art, was a slave owner's house in 1778, gives a better indication of the violence of chattel slavery than any 'killing' a film can depict. Similar places in Scotland and elsewhere in Britain, that we pass daily, have similar historical legacies and should be preserved as practical lessons of our history.

With Burns' poem about Mary Ramsay in mind, I drove, with a Scottish friend, to Ayr in 2015 to look at the Auchencruive Estate of Richard Oswald. My friend, like many Scots, has been concerned that this history is not well known in a country of 'The Enlightenment'. Auchencruive Estate and Tower, on the deaths of Richard and Mary Oswald, passed to members of the Oswald family; some gained titles and became Members of Parliament. They sold the Estate, containing House and Tower, in 1819. The purchaser bequeathed the Estate and Tower to the Secretary of State for Scotland in 1927 for use as the West of Scotland Agricultural College. This College became the Scottish Agricultural College which moved to a new site by 2007. In 2011, South Ayrshire Council approved the development of the site but in December 2012 Auchencruive House (renamed Oswald Hall) was sold for £1,500,000 to Neogen Europe to be used as corporate offices.

The entrance to the Estate was a narrow lane. The Estate contained a mixture of buildings of different styles: From cheap modern constructions to courtyard cottages to the damaged Oswald's Tower and to the grandeur of Auchencruive House with its neo-classical symmetry at the front and its open-armed-shaped black painted iron staircase at the back, which linked a large room on the first floor to a large open green lawn. I peeped through the glass of the locked front door and saw small statues in the Hall. A man called me from behind. He asked if I had permission to look through the glass. I said that I was Jamaican and that my ancestors' efforts helped to purchase this House. He then said that there is indeed a Jamaican connection because during the refurbishment, woods from Jamaican trees were used as part of the construction. I said, I hoped they were not removed and discarded…he declined to answer and returned to fixing his car.

As I walked down to the river Ayr which flows passed the House, I saw a small neat graveyard for animals that were family pets. I then remembered what Thistlewood (1721-1786) said in his notorious slave master's diary that he once heard a slave say, "If this is life then let me die." It then crossed my mind that I had never seen the grave of a chattel slave. As I walked along the bank of the river, I suddenly realised that the granite wall of the river bank was constructed to look like the wall of a castle. From the river bank, Auchencruive house appeared to be perched on the top of a castle. This wanton squander of money, earned from a cruel slavery that limited the lives of young healthy black men to less than 10 years, was a compelling but an incomprehensible folly.

Auchencruive House was in good condition but the Tower, made from granite blocks, had collapsed in certain sections. The deterioration of this Tower was of great concern to me. This monument, like the false castle wall, reflects the cruelty and the folly of chattel slavery which the local Council should have looked after for the Nation and the World. On the 17th August 2015, having noticed in the literature that Oswald's Tower was on the 'Buildings at Risk Register for Scotland', I wrote to the Chief Executive Officer of South Ayrshire Council requesting that Oswald's Temple be restored because of the international history it embodies. On the 11th of September 2015, I was pleased to receive a response which stated that the Council recognised the "historical significance" of Oswald's Tower as a "Category A listed Temple". The Council also stated that although current financial funding constraints limit the restoration of the Temple by the Council, it has "imposed a condition (number 37) on the planning permission in principle, granted in July 2012, for a proposed mixed use development of Auchencruive Estate". This order includes that "Phase C" of the development shall not commence prior to the full restoration of Oswald's Temple" and that no structures are permissible on the grassed area surrounding the Oswald's Temple building".

Nevertheless, it was concerning to me that those who have benefited from this slavery should have allowed the Temple to fall into a state of structural risk and decay. However, I am pleased that a plan exists for the restoration of Oswald Temple. The present is the future and the predictable consequences of the 'sins of our fathers' are often difficult to accept or deal with but Richard Oswald must be turning in his grave at the realisation that a descendant of slaves, from Jamaica, is trying to save his Temple as historical evidence of "Man's inhumanity to Man".

*At the completion of this article, I notice that "Ode, sacred to the memory of Mrs. Oswald of Auchencruive", by Robert Burns, was analysed by Dumfries Museum in association with Burns Scotland collections held in partnership, which is an organisation supported by Museums Galleries Scotland. In terms of what I referred to above as historical "fiction of forgetfulness" I was concerned to notice that, in the Museum's analysis, the source of the money that produced Burns' damnation of the Oswalds was not mentioned... our Chattel Slavery.

G H Palmer

Epilogue

For the future we should talk of one race...the Human race; all one people but different. About the past, we must never forget that 300 years of the most brutal slavery was based on the contrived conclusion that the black colour of the skins of African people made them inferior and ideal material for distant legal enslavement. The consequences of human prejudice are invariably cruel and nothing was crueler than labelling people Chattel and then enslaving them, without a moveable word against the wicked deed, for centuries. The consequences of slavery have made us what we have become... people affected in different ways by the most profitable evil the world has known.

Although we commemorate and learn from other atrocities, there are some who begrudge that the horrors of British slavery, which killed untold millions of defenceless black people, is being remembered in 2007. This slavery was based on skin colour. It has taken more than 200 years for black people to regain the dignity of colour they had before slavery. The source of this dignity-regained was the holocaust of Chattel slavery. From this cultural source flows a lineage from which my black identity is derived. We who are not white share this identity. Any attempt to remove this identity sanctions racism against black people.

Today, 200 years after the abolition of the slave trade, our lineage of being black is: genetic, universal and not controlled by degrees of blackness or laws. In contrast, our links to countries are historical and are affected by degrees of association and laws. Our black identity is an act of creation and cannot be changed by anyone. Therefore, for a group of white civil servants to act on the self-interest and supposed "fear of skin colour abuse" of a handful of Africans and propose replacing black and white categories on census forms with "African" and "European", is imperialistic bias taken too far. This concept of phenotype discrimination is racism by stealth and is saying that, "African" is Negroid-related and "European" is white Caucasian-related. Without a black identity, millions of people, that are neither African-Negro nor Caucasian, would lose their human identity, unity and freedom. "Apartheid purity", Negro or Caucasian, concerns me because at a recent lecture on the heroes of Jamaican slave rebellions, William Gordon, a black Jamaican of mixed race was not mentioned. Bogle, Gordon's companion in nationality, faith, war and death, was mentioned. No Jamaican, including Bogle, would find this acceptable. The history of Jamaica informs us that the bitter fruits of unfairness are poverty and violence. We came out of New World slavery as many people, now we are one. New World slavery and Africa should inspire us; we should not use them as crutches.

The white civil service system has never responded so quickly before to any of the needs of black people. Therefore, the reason for the proposed census ban on our black identity in 2007 must be seen as no better than the beads or bullets which were exchanged for slaves. We must insist that the choice to be who we say we are must remain and that black, white or any other identity must not be abolished, changed or tampered with again. It is almost unpardonable that our black identity, so dearly earned, can be put out to consultation by ignorant people. People who gang together to lie and deny the rights of others should not be in charge of other people's freedom. A census that fails to capture, honestly, the human diversity of colour, class, race and creed cannot be used to monitor equality in any community.

Equality is dependent on identifying all the people of the community, so that their needs can be met. My colour is me and I shall not favour forms that exclude my black identity. It is evident that the civil servants involved are not aware of research that shows that a black identity is related to self-esteem and positive development. The arrogance with which this assault on black identity was carried out has done untold harm to race relations and the rights of black people. The idiot that calls me black, as an insult, does me no harm...I am black. The right to call ourselves black or white is already in place on national documents and must remain.

In March 2009 I watched a friend complete the new Scottish Rehearsal Census Form. The categories black and white had been retained. Some of our institutions will not implement equality, they deceive by playing the equality game of *forum* or *commission*, which usually delivers little. However, in this case the argument for historical truth prevailed.

Bearing this in mind, it is encouraging that in Scotland the Minister of Education (Fiona Hyslop, 2008) has acknowledged that Jamaica (as did other British West Indian slave territories) contributed significantly to the economic development of Scotland and that this history must be taught. Similar government intent from the rest of the United Kingdom would do more for race relations than the usual useless "sound bites" that come from various quarters.

Those who have made it their business to deny the history of British slavery by calling it "bad history" have lost their place like the "bad disciple". It is hoped that this new acknowledgement of British slavery history will also see the end of publications such as Rosemary Goring's recent (2007) book called *Scotland the Autobiography: 2000 Years of Scottish History by Those Who Saw It Happen* that excludes the history of those who ran Scottish slavery for Scottish interests in the New World. One can only surmise that the compliments given to this book by Professor Tom Devine, the eminent Scottish historian, were not based on the completed book. Tom's recent book, *The Scottish Nation 1707 to 2007* refers to the significant contribution British slavery made to developing the economy of Scotland during the 18th and 19th centuries. Notwithstanding, it is curious that like Rosemary Goring, Tom omitted certain aspects of Scottish history which indicate that Scotland's involvement, in British slavery, was related to self-interest, not chance. For example, he referred to Article 4 of the Act of the Union. However, that part of the Article which states that, rights will be given to trade within "the dominions and plantations" was omitted. I have found many Scots keen to know about the Nation's past involvement in British chattel slavery. Therefore, it is not clear why some Scottish historians believe that only historical 'victim-hood' is likely to be accepted by the Scottish people. Indeed, only honest history is capable of making us understand the way we live.

Thankfully, in his new book, "To the Ends of the Earth Scottish Global Diaspora", Tom Devine asks the question, "Did slavery help to make Scotland great?" Although the evidence presented did not deal with the ethnicity of the 'forgotten' Scottish Diaspora in the Caribbean, the author did conclude that "the slave-based economy of the Atlantic had a powerful impact on Scottish economic growth". For example, imports into Scotland such as slave-grown tobacco, sugar, coffee and cotton and exports such as (a) Scottish linen to clothe slaves and (b)the many thousands of Scots who became wealthy from slavery facilitated industrial and social development in Scotland during the eighteenth and nineteenth centuries. Earlier (2002), Inikori had come to a similar conclusion regarding the contribution slavery made to the industrial revolution in England.

The Scottish Government is in the process of inviting members of the Scottish Diaspora to attend "Home Coming" year 2009, to celebrate the 250th anniversary of the birth of Robert Burns. There are some reports that invitations will only be sent to the North American, Australian and New Zealand Diaspora. Since Burns had a ticket to sail to Jamaica in 1786 and, as stated above, was associated with Jamaica in many ways, it will be of interest to see if the non-white Scottish Diaspora, that contributed life and work to help build Scotland, will be excluded. I am sure that the Scottish people will not accept racial bias at this historic event. Now, in terms of the recent gathering of the Scottish Caribbean Diaspora in China, it should not be overlooked that the surnames of some Caribbean athletes at the Beijing Olympics were: Burns, Thompson, Fraser, Sinclair, Stewart, Whyte, McFarlane, Walker, Simpson, Campbell-Brown, Burnett, Clarke, Wallace, Douglas, Stuart and Ferguson. Many of these athletes are from Jamaica. Other Jamaican athletes such as Usain Bolt and Asafa Powell are from Trelawny and St Catherine, respectively. Trelawny and St Catherine are Parishes in Jamaica where Scottish slave masters congregated. Lord Balcarres was made governor of Jamaica by the powerful Scottish politician, Henry Dundas (Lord Melville). Balcarres effected the defeat of the Jamaican Maroons in Trelawney in 1795. To enhance the 'efficiency' of slave plantations, many Maroons were exiled to Nova Scotia. In 1837, James Ewing from Glasgow owned a large slave (sugar) plantation called Caymanas in St Catherine. He used a portion of his vast slavery-derived wealth to build the Necropolis in Glasgow. Despite the selective reporting of Scottish Colonial history, if the "Home Coming" event is truly about Burns, an invitation should be extended to all, not some. Burn's identity extends beyond a single group of people. Henry Dundas (Lord Melville) was MP for Midlothian when he suppressed the freedom of slaves in Jamaica. Just over 200 years later Midlothian Council made me a Freeman of Midlothian. This historical irony is not only an honour to me but an honour to the Scottish Diaspora that Lord Melville helped to create. From important historical connections between Jamaica and Scotland such as inherited genes, surnames and flag design, Jamaicans may also have 'adapted' parts of the Scottish language. For example, Jamaican 'bad words' (swear words) are well known and, a related series of Jamaican 'bad words' (swear words) contain the word 'clart'. Clart could have been derived from the Scottish 'dirty' word 'clarty' many generations ago.

Social development and national identity are linked to honest history not contrived stories that insult and divide rather than please the good citizen.

The importance of this view can be found in a lecture given by Professor Tom Devine on his retirement as one of the leading historians of Scotland. Mindful of studies that have shown that Scotland played a significant part in managing British slavery in the Caribbean, Tom, with characteristic honesty (The Herald, Scotland, 21st March 2010), 'apologised for failing to focus on the shameful connections between Scotland and the slave trade'. As stated in this book some time ago, Tom now acknowledges with clarity that, "The jewel in the crown in the Caribbean was Jamaica, which was the single richest colony in the British Empire during the 18th century and that if you look at the telephone directory of Jamaica it's full of Scottish names. These are the people who have taken their names from their Scottish masters." He also stated that, like sugar and coffee from the Caribbean, tobacco from slave plantations in America contributed to the economic development of Scotland in the 18th century. At a time when there was much poverty in Scotland, he confirmed that "a lot of young Scots went out there (the Caribbean), including one Robert Burns, who was about to go out to a post in Port Antonio in Jamaica in 1786."

That references to this history were omitted from the work of many historians is difficult to explain but a large number of Scottish people are concerned that this important area of Scottish history was wiped clean from their education. However, it is important for community development that one of Scotland's leading historians has added an academic voice; to that of Scotland's Culture Secretary (Fiona Hyslop) and Education Secretary (Mike Russell) that, this history, despite its challenges, should become part of the education Scottish people need to play a positive part in the world. In this context, from a position of giving very little information about its origins in terms of slavery, the Glasgow Gallery of Modern Art has bought three silk screen linear paintings by Graham Fagen of the three ships (Nancy, Bell and Roselle) that Robert Burns was booked on to sail to Jamaica in 1786, to be a "slave driver". These historical paintings are now on exhibition in the Gallery's grand neo-classical building, built by William Cunninghame in 1778 from his vast wealth gained from his dealings in slave grown tobacco and his sugar plantation in Jamaica...a small country that once provided vast wealth to many but is now struggling alone to survive.

In contrast to the positive actions taken by Education Ministers in Scotland to add the history of Scotland's involvement in British slavery to its new Curriculum of Excellence; Michael Gove, the Education Minister of the UK government in 2013, which is the 175th anniversary of the abolition of British slavery, was on the verge of removing Black people, such as Seacole and Equiano, from the national history curriculum. Seacole and Equiano are regarded as important slavery-linked role-models in Black-British history. It is unlikely that Gove studied the history of British slavery in any depth during his school days in Scotland but it is frustrating that it took a petition signed by 36,000 people to have Seacole (see page 64) and Equiano reinstated into the national curriculum of British history. There is still the backward view in some quarters that Black-British slave history should remain hidden but this will not happen now. In this regard it is worth noting that David Cameron, the Prime Minister, has given credence to the historical importance of British Slavery by stating that the abolition of its own slavery is evidence of British (Scottish) greatness. Educationally, it is important that all the people involved in this "greatness" are given equal historical attention, in terms of contributions made to British (Scottish) societies.

The responses of the Scottish people to this poorly know Scottish-Black people history have been enlightening. Most of these Scottish people have said with great concern: "Why have we not been told about our involvement in the history of Black chattel slavery before?" However, the new Scottish Curriculum of Excellence (2012) contains sections of this history of Black chattel slavery. In 2009, the Gathering of the Scottish Diaspora was an all White people affair...in 2014 the Gathering of the Scottish Diaspora will include countries such as Jamaica. The recent official visit to

Scotland of Her Excellency, Aloun Ndombet-Assamba, the High Commissioner for Jamaica, contributed significantly to developing a two-way productive relationship in terms of trade, culture and tourism between Jamaica and Scotland. A joint past of cruelty and war has changed to a joint future of hope and respect.

For the future, we must talk honestly about our identities and our histories (and this includes Chattel slavery) so that our children will learn that racial prejudice is the dangerous lie that damages us all.

Addendum: Scottish doctors and British slavery in the Caribbean (Jamaica). Also: brief comments on the timeless slavery histories of the Lamonts and the Baillies...

Many of the young Scotsmen that travelled the long way to the Caribbean to make their fortunes from British slavery were lawyers and doctors. Slavery was as much about material property as it was about living property. Material properties were plantations and products such as sugar, tobacco and coffee. Living properties were slaves. A sick slave that could not work was a 'waste of money'. The role of doctors in the Caribbean was to ensure that slaves were fit to work. The medical skills of Scottish doctors were well recognised during slavery. They came form Universities such as Glasgow, Edinburgh, St Andrews and Aberdeen. Qualified doctors practiced together with 'quacks' but did not approve of them. Some local Scots like James Wedderburn had learned to treat various diseases and were called doctor by fellow slave masters (see below). Records show that in 1750 in Antigua of 32 doctors, 19 were Scots.

Both slaves and slave masters suffered various diseases. Doctors specialised in treating both. Jamaica was called the 'whiteman's grave'. Common diseases were: ulcers, sores such as yaws, wounds, vomiting, diarrhoea, fevers, venereal diseases and mental diseases such as 'dirt eating' among slaves (see Thomas Thistlewood's diary where the sickness and maltreatment of his slaves in Jamaica are described in dreadful detail (1750 – 1786). A 'Dr' James Wedderburn is described). Treatments of diseases included, sulphur, soot, quinine, bleeding, cow manure and opium. I contracted yaws when I was ten year's old in Jamaica. It rotted my heel and would not heal when treated with local medicines. My aunts paid a week's salary for one injection of penicillin which cured the disease.

On the plantations, doctors worked for a plantation for a fixed sum per year or on a pay per treatment basis. Some doctors worked individually or in a practice, other doctors owned their own dispensaries. Doctors often combined careers in medicine with careers as slave masters. The earning capacities of doctors varied from about £30 to £300 per year, depending on age and skill. In terms of purchasing power, James Wedderburn bought Inveresk Lodge for about £1,000 in the 1770s, it is now worth hundreds of thousands of pounds. A doctor's practice could earn about £1,000 to£1,500 per year. When the head of one such practice died he left nearly £45,000...over £4 million pounds in today's money. The wealth of doctors can be deduced from the contribution Dr Archibald Kerr made to the Royal Infirmary of Edinburgh in 1750. He left an estate of 39 slaves to provide an annual income to develop this newly formed hospital (1729).

Patronage and kinship were key factors in the dominant role Scots' doctors played in Caribbean slavery. For example, Sir Alexander Grant of Dalvey studied medicine at Aberdeen University in 1753, paid for by the notorious slave master, Sir Archibald Grant of

Monymusk and had business links with Sir James Grant of Grant of Grantoun on Spey. In turn, Walter Grant's course in medicine was paid for by Dr Sir Alexander Grant of Dalvey. Both worked as doctors in Jamaica.

One of the great distinctions of being a doctor is to be elected a Fellow of the Royal College of Physicians of Edinburgh. Some doctors in the Caribbean were Fellows and Dr William Wright, who was a prominent doctor in Jamaica, became President of this elite organisation in 1777. He donated his medical records to Kew Gardens, in London. One unforeseen and generally unknown consequence of medical practice on slave plantations was the development of Tropical medicine. Another consequence was the extensive contribution to Botanical knowledge that came from the publications of doctors who attended to slaves in the Caribbean. Botanic gardens were established in the Caribbean to grow plants that could be used to produce medicines. Professor John Hope of Edinburgh University was involved in this venture. After I gave a lecture on Scottish Caribbean (Jamaican) history to the Senior Fellows of the Royal College of Physicians in Edinburgh on the 13th October 2014, I was shown, among other books linked to Caribbean slavery, a copy of a very large and important book of the natural sciences, written by a slave doctor who practiced in Jamaica, entitled, "A civil and natural history of Jamaica" by Patrick Brownie, published in 1756. It describes Jamaica's soil, plants, fossils, insects, reptiles, vegetables, revenues, birds, fishes, produce and trade. Linnaeus, the great biologist/taxonomist, stated after reading Brownie's book that, Brownie should be, "hounoured with a golden statue" and that, "In no author did I ever quit more instructed".

The home of the Royal College of Physicians is located at 8 and 9 Queen Street in Edinburgh. The building at 9 Queen Street was built in 1844 to 1846. The building at 8 Queen Street was built in 1717. Surprisingly, 8 Queen Street is recorded in the slavery Compensation List of 1833-1834 when British slave owners received £20 million for losing their property (slaves) at emancipation. A John Blackburn of Killearn and of 8 Queen Street is recorded on the List. In 1810, he returned from Jamaica a rich man and re-built Killearn. John Blackburn is the father of the distinguished Scottish Judge Sir Colin Blackburn of Killearn.

In 2013, at one of my lectures on this history in the Border region of Scotland, an older lady took out a painting from a brown paper bag of a young man dressed in an open front Georgian Jacket. He had the gentlest of faces. She then said, "He is an ancestor of mine and he was a doctor in the Caribbean during slavery and we have benefited from his estate."

It may seem strange that doctors saved the lives of slaves for them to be worked later to death, but this is another story of our slavery that has made us what we have become.

There are many documented life narratives in the history of British Caribbean slavery. Although I have recalled a few I have found two more that illustrate why this history, although incriminating, should be taught in detail in schools. Not long ago, one of my relatives gave me a copy of an old document for my birthday. It was bought in an antique shop. To my surprise it was entitled a RECORD, The LORD ADVOCATE against JOHN LAMONT'S EXECUTORS. Although the legal purpose of the document was to decide the "amount of the estate chargeable with duty" it contained the story of the life of John Lamont and it provided further evidence of the social complexity of the involvement of Scots in British chattel slavery in the Caribbean. Although I have paid particular attention to slavery in Jamaica, this story is about British chattel slavery in Trinidad.

John Lamont was born in 1782 in Argyll. He was the illegitimate son of James Lamont of Knockdow, Argyllshire, Scotland. John Lamont's mother was Isabella Clark. Because she was regarded as "a person of inferior station", she was not considered suitable for marriage into the 'respectable Lamont family'.

After receiving his education in Scotland, John Lamont went to the British slave island of Trinidad in 1801 or 1802. Like many young Scots who went to 'better themselves' in British slave islands in the Caribbean, John Lamont worked on a slave plantation before saving enough to purchase his own plantation. In 1809, he purchased a plantation called Ceder Grove. With the money he gained from Ceder Grove he purchased La Grenade, River, Cascade and St Ellena estates. He was also the joint proprietor of the Canaan estate. He died in 1850 in Trinidad and was buried next to his brother Boyden Lamont in Trinidad.

During his time in Trinidad as a slave master, John Lamont returned to Scotland many times for short visits to bank and invest the considerable fortune he had accumulated from his slave plantations in Trinidad. During his visits to Glasgow he wrote letters from the Western Club and 39 West Nile Street (the counting house). According to his will, he left £90, 000 15s 9p which in today's money would have been equivalent to about £9,000,000. Towards the end of slavery in 1838 and up to 1847 he banked, on average, about £10, 000 per year in the Ship

Banking Company in Glasgow. He also had £40,807 5s 11p in the Glasgow based Western Bank of Scotland. His many letters to his half-brothers and business colleagues contained a detailed account of the selling of his slave-grown sugar. However, the words slave or slavery is not mentioned in John Lamont's will. In passing, the fortunes that could be gained from slavery were stated earlier by Robert Burns in his 1788 poem, *Ode to the sacred memory of Mrs Oswald of Auchencruvie*. The great disparity between the £30 annually he would have earned as a 'slave driver' and the glittering £10,000 annuity per year that Mrs Oswald received from her deceased husband, who was the notorious slave owner Richard Oswald, rankled him and he damned her to 'perdition'.

The historical home of Clan Lamont is Knockdow House (Argyll). John Lamont bought the Benmore estate for £13,000 in 1849 and he died in 1850. He left most of his money and properties in Scotland and Trinidad to members of his Lamont family...his nephew James Lamont inherited the Benmore estate and became Sir James the 1st Baronet. Benmore estate was eventually purchased by the Younger's brewing family and they donated it to the nation in 1925. Benmore estate is now named the Benmore Botanic Gardens and is located north of Dunoon in the Cowal Peninsula, Argyll and is open to the public. Recently the 113th Gathering of Clan Lamont was held in Knockdow House. John Lamont's slavery derived money has ensured that Knockdow House remains in the ownership of Clan Lamont. Sir Norman Lamont (1869-1949) inherited Knockdow House and was gored to death by his own bull on the Lamont family estate in Trinidad.

In John Lamont's letters to this brother Alexander Lamont, John Lamont wrote in a deferential manner as if illegitimacy gave him a subordinate position in the family. In contrast, in letters pertaining to goods such as sugar he was the forceful businessman of slavery, managing every penny. In parts, the narrative of the life of John Lamont reminds us that individuals in Scotland who suffered social ills, as a result of the Highland Clearances, Culloden and other National strifes, went to British slave colonies and made large fortunes by enslaving defenceless black chattel slaves. Human intent is often more difficult to understand than human error.

In general, until recently, white people of Scotland and black people of the Caribbean have found slavery an uneasy topic to discuss because slavery was portrayed as: white people dominating black people and then freeing them rather than as a long period of cruel economic exploitation, conflict and rebellion. We cannot pick and choose from the past to construct an honest historical identity. The good and the bad must to be included or we will continue to live a lie, still failing to address the racist attitudes and practices that have their origins in slavery.

John Lamont's obituary in 1850 said that he had "accumulated a very large fortune, by care, perseverance, and intelligence accompanied by the strictest integrity, and marked by honour in all his transactions". Long after British slavery was abolished in 1838, this unfortunately remains the 'enlightened view' of some who do not realise that if one benefits from the past then one has a social responsibility to acknowledge and learn from the past.

In 2004 the Government of Trinidad outlined a project to build houses on the graves of John Lamont, Boyden Lamont and Sir Norman Lamont. However, the local people of Canaan district, once part of the slave plantation empire owned by John Lamont, insisted that the graves should not be damaged and desecrated by building on them. The Government listened to the people and the graves with their headstones were saved. Here the dignity of the slave master and his family was protected by the descendants of their slaves...such is the redeeming nature of our common humanity that says we are different but we are of the same race, the human race.

Recently, I wrote an article in *The Herald* (Opinion – 9.1.2014) on the under-taught historical involvement of Scotland in British chattel slavery. In another article in this issue of the paper, I was quoted as stating that, "Scotland's involvement in slavery should be a detailed study" in schools. Such courses would improve race relations. They would also widen our historical and cultural identities. Many Scottish people have remarked that the great extent of Scottish involvement in British slavery, in the New World, is shocking and wonder why this history was not taught in any detail to them in school. It is not known why many historians have ignored this important part of Scotland's history. However, whilst the role of abolitionists in helping to abolish slavery is taught in some quarters, the significant involvement of Scottish people in this slavery, for over one hundred and fifty years, is not taught in detail.

This tendency to 'leave out' this history is illustrated in the recent obituary of Lord Burton of Dochfour (The Herald, 5.6.2013). In this obituary, mention was made of some of the ancestors of the tempestuous Lord, who 'occasionally...came into conflict with members of the public who encroached upon his property'. Lord Burton had two ancestors who were short-reigned kings of 'Old Scotland'. Also, it was stated that he inherited grand estates, including Dochfour. It was mentioned that he gained his

Lordship and some of his fortune from being the grandson of Lady Nellie Bass of the Bass brewing family. Various aspects of his life were mentioned but there was no mention that the Baillie brothers, James and Evan, were his notorious slave-owning ancestors whose properties such as Dochfour in Scotland helped to make Lord Burton of Dochfour a very rich man at birth. James Baillie MP (1792) called abolitionists, "ignorant and low men" because he felt that the slavery business of the family was being threatened by talk of abolition. The Baillies' slavery empire was mainly in St Kitts and Grenada (1765). James' brother Evan Baillie MP consolidated the slavery-earned fortunes of the family which were passed down to Lord Burton whose name was, George Evan Michael Baillie.

The history of British slavery in now an important part of Black History Month. In October 2015, it was remembered that 150 years ago the Jamaicans Bogle and Gordon initiated the Morant Bay Rebellion which improved British governance of its ex-slave colonies in the Caribbean. Like other Jamaican rebels such as Tacky (1760) and Sharpe (1832), they were hanged. Fighting and dying for human freedom should be remembered. Indeed, someone told me that Jamaica made the first contribution to support the building of spitfires, the planes that are the central focus of annual memories of the 2nd World War. Another important topic relating to Jamaica was David Cameron's first visit to Jamaica as Prime Minister. David Cameron's response to calls for an apology and reparation for British slavery was that, we should "move on" from the past. The Prime Minister did say some time ago that the abolition of British slavery in 1838 was an example of British greatness. To offer to build a £25M prison in Jamaica in 2015 as part of an aid package was regarded by many as inappropriate (The

Herald, Call for Scotland to atone for decades of slavery in Jamaica, 2nd October 2015). In this regard, a great opportunity was lost because Jamaican-British history could have been used to improve race relations. The worst sin is not contrived forgetfulness of the past or the 'historical amnesia' proposed belatedly by Scotland's premier historian, Sir Tom Devine, it is ingratitude (see Scottish Diaspora Tapestry, 2014 (23, 24).

For example, It is known that for nearly two hundred years Jamaican slaves worked as chattel slaves to build the infra-structure that made Britain rich but left Jamaica and other slave islands poor. The sadness of the offer to build Jamaica a prison in 2015 should be weighed historically against Britain's ordering two of its greatest Naval Captains, Sir George Rodney and Sir Samuel Hood, to fight to the death at the Battle of All Saintes to stop the French taking Jamaica from Britain in April 1782. Thousands died or were wounded, sadly in similar numbers to Trafalgar (1805).

In 1781 Don Francisco Saavedra said the aim of Spain and France, "Was to conquer Jamaica, the centre of the wealth and power of Great Britain in that part of the world." At the time, King George III was more concerned about losing slave islands such as Jamaica to France and Spain than the invasion of Britain because, the profits that came from slavery islands would prevent the invasion of Britain. This is our history (one history) and it cannot be changed, forgotten or "move on" from. Indeed, we are told not to forget other historical events, so why should we forget the history of our slavery?

I agree with reparations in terms of helping to develop the necessary infra-structure that will meet the socio-economic needs of British slave colonies of the past. However, I am not keen on apologies because they are often meaningless. I am a descendant of slaves… what kind of apology should I accept for my past history of which I am proud. I am proud of those who fought the best they could to give us the life we have today.

History is that permanent part of our identity from which we cannot 'move on' from to please others. The reparation movement must now develop compelling arguments to defeat not only the 'Cameron effect' but the 'Amnesia' response to our slavery, highlighted belatedly by the Scottish historian Sir Tom Devine (see above reference, The Herald). The debate regarding the illegality or legality of slavery is an unnecessary diversion. The 'European responsibility' of chattel slavery in the Caribbean is beyond dispute. This ownership, within or without the law was a breach of the rights of people to be human beings and therefore chattel slavery was a violation of human rights. The right to human life (denied to chattel slaves) supersedes all laws made by human beings.

The life lesson of our chattel slavery is important because it will remain to remind us that there are deeds for which we should surely make amends but should not have done because some deeds are beyond apologies. Finally, we cannot pick and choose from our history if we are to learn from it and widen our humanity. It is unacceptable in any society to put reputation before historical truth that develops our enlightenment.